Encounters
with
A Course in Miracles

PETER M. PARR

Copyright © 2020 Peter M. Parr

All rights reserved.

DEDICATION

To Eva

ACKNOWLEDGMENTS

I'd like to express my gratitude to:

Kitty, for your kindness, encouragement and belief in me –
and for introducing me to John Butler.

Pixabay, for the cover image.

Julie, Maria, Mike and Thom (in alphabetical order).
I'm blessed to have you as friends.

John Butler and Phil Shankland, for their YouTube videos
which helped to keep me (fairly) sane during the lockdown.

Most of all, to my mum, Eva.
You are a wonderful mum and a great teacher of the Course.

1

Eric

Eric collapsed into his armchair. Even washing-up the day's dishes and rearranging the chairs into a circle had left him exhausted. As he recovered his breath, he tried to think if he'd forgotten anything. He'd put a fresh towel in the downstairs cloakroom; clean mugs on the kitchen worktop for tea and coffee, and a plate of *Jaffa Cakes* too. Hopefully none of the group would be vegan or on a gluten-free diet. If so, he had dried apricots and some salted nuts.

The house was ready. Time, now, to prepare himself. His pain had subsided, but continued to gnaw in the background. He wondered what state he'd be in two months from now; whether he'd be able to facilitate the group. Perhaps he should have advertised it to run over six weeks rather than eight. Words from the Course came to him: *The strength the body has will always be enough to serve all truly useful purposes.*[1] He closed his eyes and began the meditation which had become his practice. In his mind, he called on Love – his source, his strength. *Love.* Let him only be aware of Its presence… Within him, surrounding him, through him. He immersed himself in its peace. *Love.* That single word prayer encompassed them all.

He jumped when his telephone rang.

Ignore it; let it ring. But it might be one of the participants, someone needing directions. Or a last-minute enquirer who'd seen the advert and wanted to know if they could still come along.

He reached for the phone and saw his daughter's name on the screen. She could have chosen a better moment to call. "Hello, darling."

"Hi dad," Emma greeted him.

"What time is it in New York? Aren't you at work?"

"I'm on my lunch break. I wanted to wish you well for tonight."

"Oh, thank you. That's kind."

"How many are you expecting?"

"There'll be seven if everyone comes."

"How are you feeling?" she asked.

"Today's not been too bad. These new pills they've given me make a difference. They knock me out, but they help."

"I worry about you, dad. You will tell me if it gets worse?"

"Yes, darling, I'll tell you."

"'Cause I want to come over and be there with you."

Eric heard the trembling in her voice. Don't start crying on me, he thought. Not now, when I've people arriving in twenty minutes and I need to be in the right place. "I'll give you a call later," he suggested. "Then I can let you know how it went."

"I love you, Dad," Emma said.

"I know you do. I love you too... Darling, people will be here in a minute..."

"Oh, right, let's speak tomorrow then. It'll be late when it finishes, and you need to get your rest. I'll Skype you in the morning before I leave for work. I'll get Danny on the call."

"That'd be wonderful. Give him a hug from his granddad."

"Will do."

"Take care," Eric said.

"*You* take care. I'll see you soon."

"Yes, see you soon." As he said that loaded word 'soon', he felt a tightness. He longed to see his daughter and grandson. But not soon. Not just yet. He knew that, when they did fly over to visit him, it would be for the final time.

He shut his eyes again and resumed his meditation. His mind kept wandering to Emma and Danny; to the future, and the past. Before long, he heard footsteps outside on the gravel path, and then the sound of the doorbell. Someone had come early – it wasn't time yet. Once again, the world held up a mirror to his thoughts.

* * *

One by one, the participants arrived. Eric greeted them, took their coats and showed them to the sitting room.

He noticed judgments springing up in his mind: 'talkative'; 'shy'; 'could do with losing some weight'. The young woman with the turquoise scarf who sat opposite him would have been his type, thirty or forty years ago. He smiled at the ridiculousness of his thoughts. His ego mind still had a foothold, labelling and pigeon-holing. At least now he could observe it consciously, and not be controlled by it. He said a silent prayer: *Help me to see my brothers and sisters as they truly are.*

The wall clock said five past seven. A couple of people had glanced at their watches. One man sat in awkward silence while others around him made small talk.

"Are we expecting anyone else?" asked Daisy, the elegant woman in her early sixties who sat to Eric's left.

"One more," said Eric. Perhaps the final person had decided not to come. After another minute or so, sensing Daisy's impatience, he decided to make a start. "Welcome everyone. Thanks for coming. My name's

Eric. I'll be focalizing this group.

"*A Course in Miracles* has been a big part of my life for the last twenty years. Over these next eight weeks we've an opportunity to explore what the Course teaches, but also to practice it. It gives me pleasure to share my experience and understanding but, for me, the real beauty of a group like this is people coming together and connecting with one another. That's all I'll say for now. Shall we go around the circle and introduce ourselves? Please say your name, and a few words about why you're here. Who would like to start?"

"Hello everyone. I'm Daisy. I came across the Course six months ago and I've been doing the lessons. I'm up to Lesson 97 – I've fallen a little behind. When I heard about this group and saw the address was in Devonshire Road I took it as a sign to come along. I was born in Devon, you see!"

"Thank you, Daisy," said Eric. He signalled to the next person to go ahead.

"I'm Irene. I go to the same yoga class as Daisy. I'm not very familiar with the book but Daisy finds it helpful and recommended it, so I'm here to discover more."

"Welcome, Irene," Eric said.

"I'm Katie," the woman in the turquoise scarf introduced herself. "I teach music in a secondary school. I also play the violin, which is my first love. I've been studying the Course on and off for three years. Sometimes it speaks to me more than anything else I've come across. Other days I feel like throwing it across the room!"

"I've felt like that too!" said the man next to her. "Geoff. I'm also a teacher, but PE. What else to say? I want to meet other people who are trying to live more consciously. I find the Course challenging. I've given up with it a couple of times, but I keep coming back."

"Thank you, Geoff." Eric invited the man next along to introduce himself.

"People call me Rav," the man said quietly. Eric was glad he'd sat nearby, or he might not have been able to hear him. "I am not a student of *A Course in Miracles*, but I have read a little about this teaching. I follow advaita vedanta. It feels to me like there are many similarities. I'm here to listen and I hope to learn."

"Would you like to say a bit about advaita, for those who may not be familiar with it?"

Unlike the others, Rav seemed comfortable with maintaining eye contact. Almost imperceptibly, he bowed his head. "When I look at you, and you look at me, we see the same Self. This, for me, is advaita."

Eric felt humbled. What a gift!

"Shall I go on?" Another voice brought him back to the room.

"Yes, please," said Eric.

"My name's Mark. I've been with the Course for about seven years. I liked what Rav said. I know *theoretically* that we're all one, but how can I *live* that belief? I feel like Jekyll and Hyde. It's easy enough to remember who I am when I'm sat on my own at home, reading the Course. But when I'm at work, or under pressure, it goes out the window. I want to be able to stay centred all of the time."

"Thank you, Mark, for your openness. Thank you everyone. I'm sure that, over these next few weeks, we'll all be able to learn a lot from one another. I heard that there are at least two teachers in the room but, in fact, we're all teachers. Every day, without knowing it, we're teaching the world about who we think we are and who others are for us.

"Now, before we go any further, I'd like us to agree some ground rules; a charter, if you like, for our time together, so our group is a safe and fruitful space. Would anyone like to suggest some guidelines?"

"Arrive and start promptly," said Daisy. "I can't stand it when people are late."

"Okay," said Eric. "Can we all agree to make an effort to get here on time? Sometimes we'll begin with a meditation. If people arrive after we've begun, it might disturb others. And if you *are* going to be a few minutes late – or if you're not able to come to one of the sessions, do please let me know. Have you all got my number or my email?"

People nodded.

"Right, what else?"

Daisy spoke again. "Switch off mobile phones."

Eric realised that he hadn't put his on silent. "Great reminder," he said. "And, you know what? I'd forgotten about mine! That could have been embarrassing if it rang during a meditation," he added. He retrieved his phone and turned it off completely to avoid fiddling about with the settings. "Are there any other ground rules we'd like to adopt?" He looked across the room, away from Daisy, so she'd give other people a chance to make suggestions.

"Confidentiality," said Mark.

Eric nodded, glad that suggestion had come from the group. "Would you like to say more?"

"Whatever people share should remain…" The sound of the doorbell interrupted him. "…Should remain within the group."

"Absolutely. We want this to be a place where it's safe to share from our own experiences. Excuse me for a moment," Eric said, getting up and going to the hall. He opened the front door and saw a young man who couldn't be much over twenty, with dreadlocks and a stud in his nose. He hadn't met a white man with dreadlocks before.

"Christopher," the guy introduced himself, holding out a tattooed hand. "Is this the right place for the Miracles group?" A public schoolboy accent belied his appearance, surprising Eric again.

"Yes, do come in." Eric became aware of his

judgments and fears that this person might be disruptive. *I trust my brother, who is one with me*, he prayed silently.[2] "We're through there in the sitting room… Oh… Would you mind taking off your shoes please?"

"They're not muddy," said Christopher, facing Eric.

Eric motioned, apologetically, to where the others had left their trainers or shoes. He realised in that moment what a pointless house rule it was… a leftover from when he'd still been married. Chloe had been obsessive-compulsive when it came to dirt. He was about to say 'don't worry', but Christopher pulled off his trainers and chucked them among the rest.

"We're just agreeing to some ground rules," said Eric.

Christopher strode into the room and made for the remaining untaken chair, between Eric's and Daisy. Poor Daisy looked horrified.

"This is Christopher." Eric returned to his seat. "Mark, you were talking about the importance of confidentiality. Would you repeat what you were saying?"

"Just that, if people share anything personal, we should keep it within the group."

"Absolutely. But also, we'll sometimes divide into smaller groups or pairs. Can we agree, too, that anything we say there remains between the speaker and the listeners? We won't bring back to the wider circle what another person has shared. Does everyone agree?" He looked around the room, checking in with everyone. "Good," he said. "Have we missed anything? How else can we make this a safe space?"

"By showing respect for one another," offered Rav. "We may have different perspectives, but it's important to listen with an open mind."

"That's another very important one. Listening is a skill, and it takes practice. Often in conversations, we're not focused on the speaker, but are thinking about what we're going to say next, and waiting for an opportunity to jump in. My suggestion, if you're willing to try it, is to leave a gap after someone else has finished speaking before coming in with thoughts of your own. Also, try to give everyone a chance to share. If you've already spoken, think twice before coming in for a second time, until everyone who wishes to say something has had the chance." He looked at Daisy, then around the circle, so she wouldn't get the impression he'd singled her out. "This isn't a discussion group… we don't have to convince other people. We may not agree with one another about everything, but that's okay."

"Maybe they should try following these rules in the House of Commons," said Geoff.

"Well, it would certainly be interesting to see what would happen if they did!" Eric paused, giving space in case anything else needed to be said. "A key part of the practice of *A Course in Miracles* is listening to the Holy Spirit, to our Inner Guide. We're going to struggle to do that if we're not even able to listen to one another. That reminds me of another thing… Language.

"The Course uses some religious-sounding language – words like 'Christ', 'forgiveness', even 'miracle' – though, as we'll discover, it interprets those words in an unfamiliar way. I'll explain their distinctive meanings as we go along. Remember, words are only symbols. They point beyond themselves, so don't make them into barriers. If I talk about the Holy Spirit, for example, and that doesn't resonate, translate it into language that does… Maybe Inner Guide or, as my Quaker friends might say, 'the promptings of love and truth in your heart'.[3]

"As Rav says, treat one another with respect and consideration… With love. Everything else flows from that." Eric drank from his glass of water and took a moment to sense whether the activity he had in mind was still the right thing to do.

"We've spoken about the value of listening," he said.

"I'd like us to spend a few minutes now listening to one another. For this, we'll work in pairs."

People exchanged nervous glances.

"I'd like you to talk about a time when you extended love to someone else. It might have been a relative, a friend, or a stranger. Recall an occasion when you acted in a kind or loving way without hoping for anything in return. I'd also like you to share how you felt afterwards." Eric glanced around the circle. He could be mischievous and pair Christopher with Daisy, but perhaps better not at this first session. "Mark and Rav, would you pair up for this? Geoff and Katie, would you work together? Irene and Daisy? Christopher, are you happy to work with me?"

"How long have we got?" asked Daisy.

"Let's say three minutes each, one person talking and the other simply listening. Then swap over. When you're the listener, resist any urge to comment or ask questions. Try to maintain eye contact if you can."

Christopher sat with his arms crossed.

"Would you like to begin?" Eric asked him.

"I'm not sure I can think of anything. You go first."

"Okay," said Eric. "I'll share an experience I had yesterday in the supermarket. I'd ticked off all the items on my shopping list – at my age, I need a list or I end up forgetting half of what I went there to buy. I had the idea to treat myself to my favourite dark chocolate, but when I got to the confectionary aisle, I found the shelf almost empty. They had the chocolate bars on offer – 50 pence off – but there were only two left. I put them in my trolley, thinking I'd take advantage of the special deal – but then another thought came to me. If I bought them both, there'd be none left for the next person. Someone else would be disappointed. I decided to put one of the bars back. The instant I made that choice, I felt lighter and happier."

Christopher grinned. "When you said, 'talk about

showing love for another person', I thought you meant something big. That's why I didn't know what to say. But, yeah, if you mean small acts of kindness…"

"Is there one you'd like to share?"

"Sure. A few months ago, I found a ten pound note on the street. Rather than spend it on beer, I bought some cereal for the food bank. I opened the box and left the ten pound note inside, then resealed it. If someone has to rely on the food bank, they could use that money more than me."

What a perfect demonstration of kindness from this brother who Eric had been quick to judge. "That's beautiful. What gave you the idea?"

Christopher shrugged. "I found the tenner on my way to the shop. Then I noticed the box where people leave food donations. I could have bought a load of canned veg and pasta like I sometimes do, but hiding the money seemed more fun… I imagined a mum opening the box and finding it, and it brightening her day."

"I'm sure it did," said Eric. "And yours as well?"

"Yeah, mine as well."

Eric thanked Christopher and turned his attention back to the group. He sensed a real buzz around the room. He let them continue their conversations for a bit longer before calling time. "Would anyone like to share how you felt after your kind deed?"

"Wonderful!" said Daisy. "It lifted my spirits, and the other person's too."

"I felt great," chipped in Katie.

"When I do something that makes another person happy, that's when I feel happiest," said Mark.

"You may not realise it," Eric said, "but you've just been talking about miracles. At its simplest, a miracle is an expression of love." He saw surprised looks on people's faces. "We tend to think of miracles as supernatural acts which overturn the laws of nature. At the very least, they're dramatic events. But, in the

Course, a miracle is any expression of love. It's an act of joining with another person, a demonstration that your interests are one with theirs."

"So *A Course in Miracles* is really about love?" asked Irene.

"In a sense," said Eric. "It's about rediscovering what we are. It's about reclaiming love as our natural state of being."

"Does that mean you won't be teaching us how to turn water into wine?" Christopher joked.

"Not tonight," said Eric. "Having said that, miracles *do* transcend the world's laws." He picked up the sheet he'd prepared with quotations from the Text. "Listen to this: *'Miracles are a kind of exchange. Like all expressions of love, which are always miraculous in the true sense, the exchange reverses the physical laws. They bring more love both to the giver and the receiver.'* [4] That's from Chapter 1 of the Text: Principles of Miracles. The world's laws tell us that when we give something to another person, we lose what we've given. Expressions of love are different. When I offer love, my awareness of love increases. I expand. I feel more fully alive."

"Is love the same as kindness?" asked Katie. "I find love a difficult word."

"In what way, difficult?" Eric asked.

"For a start it's overused. People say they love someone, but what they're really talking about is need. With genuine kindness, there are no strings attached."

"True," said Eric. "Though when we speak about miracles, we're referring to unconditional expressions of love. Here's another of the Principles: *'Miracles are habits, and should be involuntary. They should not be under conscious control. Consciously selected miracles can be misguided.'*" [5] Eric paused, inviting the group to ponder. He wanted them to become more comfortable with silence.

"I'm not sure I get that one," said Geoff.

"What do you think it might mean?" Eric asked him.

Geoff looked up, as though seeking inspiration. "We shouldn't consciously plan miracles. They should come through us, not from us, maybe?"

"That's a good way of putting it. If we make a conscious decision to be kind or loving, we could have an ulterior motive. We might be expecting or hoping for something in return. If so, our action would be 'misguided' – which means guided by our ego, rather than inspired by the Voice for God, or love. When we offer miracles spontaneously, they're expressions of our deepest Self. We don't think about breathing, or count the cost. We simply breathe. Expressions of love are the same." Eric stopped to give them a chance to absorb what he'd said.

Almost immediately, Daisy broke the silence. "Sometimes we're kind to someone and they don't acknowledge it. In fact, they're ungrateful."

"It may appear that way," Eric said. "But the Course assures us, even if they don't have observable effects, miracles are never in vain: *'A miracle is never lost. It may touch many people you have not met, and produce undreamed of changes in situations of which you are not even aware.'* [6] Expressions of love create ripples in the pool of life. Have you ever let someone out in front of you in traffic?"

Daisy nodded.

"Have you noticed what happens afterwards?" he asked her.

"They sometimes flash their taillights to say thank you. Not always though."

Eric continued. "When I'm driving, if I let someone go in front me, they often 'pass it on'. They stop to let someone out in front of them. Kindness is highly contagious. We have no idea what knock on effects our expressions of love may have."

"We're doing the Principles of Miracles in Chapter 1, right?" asked Mark. He had his copy of the Text open on his lap. "Can you explain number 24?"

"Would you like to read it out?" Eric asked.

"*'Miracles enable you to heal the sick and raise the dead because you made sickness and death yourself, and can therefore abolish both.* You *are a miracle, capable of creating in the likeness of your Creator. Everything else is your own nightmare, and does not exist. Only the creations of light are real.'"*[7]

"This is getting quite deep into the theology of *A Course in Miracles.*" Eric waited, handing the question over to his Inner Guide. "We're told in this passage, 'You are a miracle', an expression of love. That's because our Creator is God, and God *is* Love. We're then told that we're capable of creating in the likeness of our Creator. The words 'create' and 'make' have particular meanings in the Course. What's 'made', is made up. In other words, it's not real. Only what's created is real.

"When the Course refers to 'creations', it's saying two things. First, that those things come from God, either directly, or through His creations. Second, that they share God's qualities, as God only creates in His own likeness.

"Sickness and death are not in God's likeness, since God is Spirit and doesn't get ill or die. What isn't *like* God can't be *from* God. And if it isn't from God, it can't be true." Eric caught Mark's eyes. "That's why the Course tells us, *'you made sickness and death yourself'.* They appear very real in our worldly experience, but that doesn't mean they *are* real. They're *'our own nightmare'*, nothing more."

"So we *can* experience physical healing?" asked Christopher.

"We can wake from our nightmare," said Eric. "When we waken, we know we are safe. The Course doesn't aim to heal the body. It's not the body we need to mend, but our mistaken belief that we *are* a body. It's our *mind* that we're aiming to heal. Lesson 140 of the Workbook is all about this. As long as we believe in the reality of the body, we'll think we're separate from one another and apart from God. In that state, we feel lonely and unsafe. We might bury those feelings deep in our unconscious, but a lack of ease is inevitable. And what do we call illness? Disease. Dis-ease.

"To heal means to make whole. That's the root of the word. When our minds are restored to awareness of their wholeness, their oneness – not a fleeting glimpse, but full awareness – we'll no longer be attached to our body because we'll know what we are in truth. We may experience physical healing – it's entirely possible. But whether we do or not, we'll be at peace. As the Course says in its Introduction, *'Nothing real can be threatened. Nothing unreal exists.'*[8] When we get that, I mean really *get* that..." He pointed to his heart. "We'll experience the peace of God."

2

Geoff

Geoff arrived at Eric's house bang on seven o'clock. He could see through the window that most of the others were already there. Spotting Katie among them, he smiled. The seat next to hers looked free. He pressed the doorbell, then, after waiting a bit, tapped the brass door knocker. His hands were freezing after the brisk walk from the tube.

Hearing footsteps, he glanced over his shoulder and saw that guy with the ludicrous hair.

"Hi, Geoff," the hippy called. "How's it going?"

"Hello," Geoff replied. He couldn't remember the bloke's name. Before he could say anything further, Eric opened the door.

"Ah, two for the price of one! Welcome," Eric greeted them. "Excellent, we've a full house."

Geoff wrenched off his shoes without untying their laces, keen to grab the chair next to Katie before the hippy took it. Still in his jacket, he entered the room and found her chatting with Daisy. When she saw him she waved hello.

"Hi, Katie," he said. "Hello, Daisy."

Daisy got up and gave him a perfunctory embrace and a peck on the cheek.

Katie remained in her seat. "I'm sorry, I'm awful

when it comes to names… Is it Geoff?"

His deflation became glee when she remembered. "Right first time! How's your week been?"

"Good, thanks. Pretty hectic. I've a concert coming up next month, so I've been practising most evenings."

"Concert?"

"I play in an orchestra."

"Ah, yes. The violin, isn't it?"

"You've a good memory," she said.

"I used to play the piano," Daisy joined the conversation. "At school and before I got married. I had a natural talent for it, my tutor said. I'm sorry I stopped playing."

"You could take it up again," said Katie.

"Do you know, I'd love to, I was thinking about it only last week. But there isn't the space in my room. I'd have to get rid of the dining table – it's too large, but it used to be my mother's, so it doesn't feel right to let it go."

Suddenly warm, Geoff removed his jacket and was about to hang it on the back of the chair when Katie stopped him. "I'm sorry," she said. "I think that seat's taken."

He noticed the glass of water and copy of the Course on the floor by the chair.

"That one's free." Katie pointed to a chair on the other side of the room.

"Thanks." He loitered for a moment, but unable to think of anything else to say and feeling embarrassed, he retreated to the vacant place.

* * *

Eric didn't announce the start of the meditation. He simply became still in his armchair, palms open in his lap, and closed his eyes.

Daisy continued to babble. "Where's your concert

being held?"

"At the Royal Festival Hall," said Katie.

"Is it? Wow! Have you played there before?"

"This will be my second time." Some might have called Katie's voice squeaky, but Geoff found it endearing.

"When's it happening?" asked Daisy.

"The nineteenth of November." Her words faded to a whisper as she noticed everyone had gone quiet. "Sorry," she apologized, "I didn't realize we'd begun."

"You must let me have the details," Daisy said. "I love a good night out."

When she finally stopped talking and settled, Geoff also closed his eyes. He'd had a stressful day, not helped by having to stay late to mind a detention class. How pointless is classroom detention. It's not even a deterrent. Why not make them do something useful, like paint over the graffiti in the toilets, or do boot camp circuits.

"'*I rest in God*'," said Eric.[9]

Geoff realized his mind had wandered and made an effort to focus on his breath. An image came to him: a young boy resting in the open palm of God – the picture on his nan's living room wall. His family hadn't been religious. But thinking about that picture, perhaps his nan did have faith in God. He thought of her. Resting in peace, now. And her tortoiseshell cat, Harvey, which he used to chase.

"'*I rest in God*'," Eric repeated. "'*This thought will bring to you the rest and quiet, peace and stillness, and the safety and the happiness you seek.*'"[10]

Geoff's eyes flickered open and lighted on Katie, directly opposite him. *The happiness you seek.* A twirl of her auburn hair cascaded down one side of her face.

"'*I rest in God. This thought has the power to wake the sleeping truth in you, whose vision sees beyond appearances to that same truth in everyone and everything there is…*'"[11]

He closed his eyes again, but still saw Katie, her porcelain features morphing into the face of an actress he'd had a crush on as a teen.

"*Here is the end of suffering for all the world, and everyone who ever came and yet will come to linger for a while. Here is the thought in which the Son of God is born again, to recognize himself.*"[12]

Eric's voice was slow and soothing, like his nan's. He'd let her read him bedtime stories, even when he'd outgrown them, for the tingles her voice gave him. Later, when she'd moved to Bexhill and he'd visited as a teen, he'd been so bored. Now what he wouldn't give to see and hear her again. He'd ask her questions... What had it been like to grow up without her parents? To lose them both within a few months, her dad in a U-boat strike, her mum in an air raid... How could she still have a faith after that?

"*I rest in God. Completely undismayed, this thought will carry you through storms and strife, past misery and pain, past loss and death, and onwards to the certainty of God. There is no suffering it cannot heal. There is no problem that it cannot solve. And no appearance but will turn to truth before the eyes of you who rest in God.*"[13]

* * *

"...And now, gently, whenever you are ready, open your eyes."

Geoff didn't want to the meditation to end. He heard people shuffling in their chairs, and sensed the person next to him stretch. He continued to sit with his eyes closed, calm and at peace.

"What a wonderful meditation," he heard a woman say, not Katie or Daisy. "Where is it taken from? I want to make a note."

"Lesson 109 of the Workbook," Eric replied.

Geoff moved his fingers and toes, took a deep breath

and reluctantly opened his eyes. He saw Eric pick up an embroidered yellow pouch.

"In a moment," said Eric, "I'm going to pass this bag around the circle. I'd like you each to take an object from it. No peeking inside!"

Geoff expected Eric to hand him the bag, but instead he passed it the other way, to the chubby woman with the frizzy hair. He watched her pick an object – some kind of stone. The bag made its way around the circle. Katie took a pebble from it and placed it on her thigh above the ripped knee of her jeans. Finally, the bag came to Geoff. He slipped his hand inside and alighted on two pebbles – a small, jagged one and a larger stone. He let the smaller go and returned the bag to Eric.

The stone he'd picked was mottled, dark grey with patches of orangey brown. Similar colours to Harvey, Nan's cat which he'd been thinking of earlier.

"Now, sit with the object you've chosen," Eric instructed. "Take your time to explore it, with your eyes and with your hands. Don't label it. Don't attempt to define it or compare it with anything else. Open your mind and your heart to it. Ask it what it is."

Geoff examined his stone more closely. Its colours formed blotches, continents of orange on an ocean of grey. One or the other colour predominated, depending on which side he looked at. In places, a lighter pinewood colour formed a border between the orange and the black. He gripped the pebble tight in a fist, then opened his hand and observed it in his palm. Lifting it up again, it felt smooth to touch, but not polished… He held the two ends in a pincer between his thumb and index finger, and rotated it with his other hand. Superficial scars dotted its surface, abrasions and barely visible indentations. Within the almost black areas were specks of lighter grey.

"Would anyone like to share what came up for them during that activity?" Eric asked after a minute or two.

"I never knew a pebble could be so beautiful!" Katie said. "I noticed things I'd usually have missed. All the intricate details."

"Me too," said Mark. "But I found it difficult not to describe or assess what I saw. All these adjectives kept coming into my mind."

"I'm afraid my stone was very plain," said Daisy. "Perhaps I'm missing the point, but the exercise felt a bit like navel-gazing."

"Would anyone else like to share?" Eric asked. "Rav?"

The Indian gentleman regarded a miniature spiral shell in his palm. "I allowed myself to be fully present. I didn't pre-judge what I saw, but viewed the object with fresh eyes."

"With fresh eyes," Eric repeated. "That's a good way of putting it." He addressed the group: "You can keep your object if you'd like to, as a little reminder that we can look at things in a different way. Or you can return it, if you prefer."

Geoff took his cue from Katie and hung on to his stone. Only Daisy gave hers back.

"Have a read through the titles of the first fifty workbook lessons," Eric said. "The word 'see' is in nearly half of them. The lessons aim to bring about a change in the way we see. They guide us from erroneous perception to what the Course calls 'vision'. If we mastered these opening lessons, we'd offer miracles to everyone we saw."

Eric winced as he stood up. He collected sheets of paper from the table and moved gingerly around the circle, handing one to each person. When he sat back in his chair he held his side. "Geoff," he said, "Would you like to read the first two lines?"

"Lesson 1: *Nothing I see... means anything.*' Lesson 2: *I have given everything I see... all the meaning that it has for me.*'"

"If I gave you a word," said Eric, "and asked you to

write the first five things you associate with it, I can more-or-less guarantee you'd all come up with a different list."

"Can we try it?" said Daisy.

"Would you like to?" Eric checked in with the group.

"Yes please," said Katie. Others nodded too.

"Does everyone have a pen with them?" Eric asked.

Geoff reached into his pocket and pulled out a biro. The others scrabbled about in their bags.

"On the back of your piece of paper, write the first five words that come to your mind when I say 'table'. What associations does it bring up? Just five things. Don't think about it too hard…"

Geoff jotted a couple of words, then paused before coming up with two more.

"Are you all finished?"

"Not yet!" shrieked Daisy.

Geoff added a final word.

"No peeping at your neighbours' lists," said Eric. "Time's up. Pens down!"

The hippy gave Geoff a nudge in the arm. "It's like being back at school." From his deadpan expression, Geoff couldn't tell if he meant it as a joke.

"Irene," Eric said to the tubby woman who sat to the other side of him, "Would you read out your list?"

"Me? Oh, okay… Dinner. Family. Tablecloth. Mahogany. Food."

Eric looked around the circle. "Put your hands up if you had all of Irene's words. No one? What about four of them?"

People glanced at one another.

"Three?"

Still no one raised a hand.

"Two words?"

Geoff raised his arm.

"Which words did you have in common with Irene?" Eric asked him.

"Dinner and food."

"A man after my own heart! Who had one of Irene's words?"

Three more people raised a hand.

"Geoff, as a reward for winning tonight's lingo bingo, you can nominate someone else to read their list."

Geoff smirked. "I'll go for… Katie!"

She gave him a pout, followed by a smile. "I wrote kitchen, classroom, eating, coffee and flowers."

"Who had all of those?" asked Eric.

"I had flowers," Daisy said when no one put up their hand.

"What that activity demonstrates is that even a simple thing like a table means different things to different people," said Eric. "We're seeing the world through the filter of our own past experiences and learnings. But if we all see things differently, how can those things mean anything in themselves? Lesson 51, the first of the review lessons, explains what's going on: *'I have judged everything I look upon, and it is this and only this I see. This is not vision. It is merely an illusion of reality, because my judgments have been made quite apart from reality.'* [14] Or, to rephrase that, they've been made apart from love."

"Can we play your bingo again with another word?" asked the hippy. "I'd like to suggest we try it with 'Brexit.'"

Eric grinned. "I think, Christopher, we better leave that one for another evening. But you're right, when it comes to beliefs, the differences in how we view things can be even more pronounced. Our beliefs make up our sense of self, so if you challenge my strongly held convictions, I'm likely to perceive it as an attack on me." He glanced down at his sheet. "Which leads us nicely to the next quote. Would you read it out?"

Christopher read, "Lesson 4. *'These thoughts do not mean anything…'* Lesson 11. *'My meaningless thoughts are showing me a meaningless world.'*"

"What that's telling us," said Eric, "is that the world we see is an out-picturing of our thoughts. And since our thoughts don't mean anything, neither does the world we perceive."

"I don't understand," interrupted Daisy. "Why don't my thoughts mean anything?"

"Let's take a step back. The Course uses the term 'God' as a way to describe Ultimate Reality. Ultimate Reality is Oneness." Eric continued, "But when we draw a dividing line between ourselves and what we're viewing; when our thoughts spring from a state of mind where we believe we're separate from God and from one another, we're denying Oneness. We're thinking apart from God.

"When the Course speaks about meaningless thoughts, it's referring to thoughts which deny reality and act as blockers to love.

"An analogy would be the static you hear on a poorly tuned radio. The static is meaningless. All it does is make it harder for you to enjoy the music, or listen to the voice you'd hear if you properly tuned in. The thoughts we think apart from God – ego thoughts, you could call them – are no more than static. They get in the way of what we actually *want* to hear and see. What characterises ego thoughts is some form of judgment, even if it's as subtle as labelling something with a name."

Daisy stopped him. "But if I call you Eric, that's not a judgment. Are you saying we shouldn't use names?"

"By all means, use them. We need to, to function in this world. But when you see 'Eric', do you see me as I am? Or do you see the story you've made up about this rather odd fellow, Eric, who you may or may not like, but who you view as separate from yourself?"

"Oh, we *do* like you," said Daisy.

"But if I did something objectionable, if I said something unkind, would you see me in the same light?"

"I suppose it depends," she replied.

"Christ's vision would," Eric said.

"You say our thoughts are meaningless," said Geoff, "but when we act on them they have effects?"

"If we dwell on our thoughts, never mind act on them, they affect what we see," said Eric. "But do they affect reality? Rav, would you read out the title of Lesson 14?"

"*'God did not create a meaningless world.'*"

"Can you speak up please?" asked Daisy.

Rav repeated, a little louder, "*'God did not create a meaningless world.'*"

"This is where it gets radical," said Eric. "The world appears to be a meaningless place. We see wars, illness, natural disasters. People and animals suffer and die. It's a bleak picture that leaves us questioning 'why'?" He paused before continuing. "The world we perceive witnesses to separation. That's precisely what it was made to do… The world was made as an attack on Oneness. It arose from 'a tiny, mad idea', as the Course calls it, that we – a part of God, a thought within God's mind – could somehow be separate from the Whole. [15] First, there's the thought of separation. From that, separate forms arise – people and planets and the world we perceive with our physical senses.

"Let's break it down into steps. God is the source of all that is real. Are you with me so far?"

Geoff nodded.

"God, Who is Love, creates only like Himself. And what doesn't arise from God can't exist in reality. Thoughts that we're separate, or sinful, or anything less than whole don't come from God. If we accept that, those thoughts can't be real. And what isn't real can have no effect on reality. The world we perceive is built on meaningless thoughts of separation. But neither our thoughts nor their effects alter the truth of what we are, or make the slightest dent in God's love. You're right on one level though. In the dream, our thoughts have tremendous effects."

"So *A Course in Miracles* teaches that the world is an illusion?" asked Katie.

Geoff sat up. She'd raised his main problem with the Course.

Eric closed his eyes for a moment before he answered. "Yes, but for me that's not where to begin. For most people struggling with life situations, it's too big a leap. Besides, it's possible to believe, intellectually, that the world is an illusion – and still not see truly, with the eyes of Love. As long as our perception remains unaltered, it would be nothing but a concept. The Course focuses on helping us to lift the blinkers that prevent us from seeing truly. It tells us, *'There is another way of looking at the world.'*

"That's the title of Lesson 33. I'd like to share some background to this one," said Eric. "It's the start of the story of how the Course came into being. Helen Schucman, the scribe, experienced fraught relationships with her work colleagues, in particular with Bill Thetford, the head of her department. Finally, the angst became too much for Bill. He announced to Helen that he'd had enough of the angry and aggressive feelings, and said to her, 'there must be another way'. Helen agreed and said she would help him to find it.

"The Course shows us that other way. Seeing things differently has nothing to do with the body's eyes. We're not asked to squint, or buy ourselves a new pair of glasses. To see the world differently, we need to begin in our minds, with our thoughts. Katie, please read the next line on your sheet."

"Lesson 23. *'I can escape from the world I see by giving up attack thoughts.'*"

"Here we have our roadmap. An attack thought is anything which judges a part of the Whole as sinful or less worthy of love. In this world, we all have attack thoughts, but we don't need to hold on to them. We can hand them over to the Holy Spirit and let Him offer us another perspective.

"Whenever you notice attack thoughts arising, pause. What does the Voice of Love say? Stop what you're doing. Take a moment, an hour, a day – as long as it takes for your mind to settle so you hear the Voice for God. It speaks to you, but you need to give it space. You have to be willing to hear it."

"And if we can't hear it?" asked Mark. "In the heat of the moment?"

"Any time you are tempted to curse someone, refrain from doing anything that would harm another or yourself. Realize your thoughts of condemnation can only bring you pain. Ask for help in replacing them with thoughts that will bring you peace. As Lesson 54 puts it, *'Neutral thoughts are impossible because all thoughts have power. They will either make a false world or lead me to the real one. But thoughts cannot be without effects. As the world I see arises from my thinking errors…'* – belief in separation and in the reality of sin and guilt – *'so will the real world rise before my eyes as I let my errors be corrected.'*[16]

"The word 'let' turns up all through the Course. We mightn't even notice it, but it's absolutely key. This isn't about doing something by our own effort. It's about the willingness to step back from our thoughts of judgment and allow ourselves to be led. It's about returning to our natural state and allowing love to flow through us without interference. Remember our radio analogy?

"Daisy, would you read out the next two lines please?"

"Where are we up to?"

"Lesson 20," said Eric.

"Lesson 20. *'I am determined to see.'* Lesson 21. *'I am determined to see things differently.'*"

"When we say we're determined to see, we're acknowledging that at the moment we don't see truly. We're also making a commitment to do what it takes so we *can* see. If an alcoholic is determined to be sober, what should he do?"

"Stop drinking alcohol," said Christopher.

"Exactly. As long as he drinks, he won't be sober," said Eric. "And to keep him focussed on his goal he might attend an AA support group. For us who are determined to have vision, we need to give up the unforgiving thoughts which prevent us from seeing our brothers and sisters as they really are. And, like the recovering alcoholic, we don't have to do this on our own. It's much easier, in fact it's only possible, when we turn to the Holy Spirit for support.

"In the next lesson, *'I am determined to see things differently',* we express our willingness to let our thoughts – the pictures of people and situations which we've formed in our minds – be transformed by the Voice for God. I'd like to read a couple of sentences from the Text. They're from Chapter 20, Section Seven:

"*'Your question should not be, "How can I see my brother without the body?" Ask only, "Do I really wish to see him sinless?"* ... *For what the seeing look upon is sinless. No one who loves can judge, and what he sees is free of condemnation. And what he sees he did not make, for it was given him to see, as was the vision that made his seeing possible.'* [17] The eyes of love do not condemn. Do you wish to see your neighbour as sinless? Or do you still cherish grievances and want to make the other person 'wrong'? There's a line in the Text: Would you rather be right or be happy? [18] It's really the same question. We can't have vision without forgiveness.

"Now, Irene, would you read out the final Lesson on your sheet, please?"

"Lesson 27. *'Above all else I want to see.'*"

"Right now, above all else I want some tea," said Christopher.

Geoff chuckled.

Eric laughed too. "Hang in there. It's nearly time for

our break… Now, it's one thing to say we want to see, or to see things differently. But to want it above all else? More than the promotion we've been chasing at work? More than to meet Miss or Mr Right and fall in love and live happily ever after? More, even, than a hot cup of tea and a chocolate digestive? That's a bit of a stretch!

"But, in the depths of our being, Christ's vision *is* what we want most of all. Seen through the eyes of love, there are only expressions of love or calls for love from those who have forgotten what they are. Everything is innocent. Everything is worthy, for everything is One.

"Listen to someone who's had a peak experience, maybe a near death experience, where they've felt at one with everything. They'll tell you, nothing this world can offer comes remotely close to the sense of peace and bliss that true vision brings. In the Bible, a parable likens the kingdom of heaven to a pearl of great value.[19] When the merchant found the pearl, he sold everything he had so he could buy it. That passage is pointing to the same truth as Lesson 27 in the Course. Christ's vision takes us to the door of the kingdom of heaven. From there we can look on whatever we perceive – all situations and events – yet feel the peace of God.

"When we finally realise that thinking as the ego would have us think, seeing the guilt the ego would have us see – is the cause of our pain, we'll make a free choice to see another way. God doesn't force vision upon us. But would God, Who is Love, withhold joy and peace from His child who asks? As soon as we want it above all else, vision dawns. Our darkened glasses are lifted, and we see the Light that was there all along."

3

Mark

Mark's watch had slipped around his wrist. He adjusted it so the face pointed towards him and tightened the strap a notch. Five past seven. Katie obviously wasn't coming.

The other participants were chatting like they'd known each other for years. The two older women, Daisy and the plump one, chirruped away... "Lou's not a bad instructor, but I prefer Samantha. She's more present, don't you think? She saw me struggling with the camel pose and came over to help. Lou just leaves you to it." No way into that conversation, thought Mark.

He glanced at Rav and the PE teacher. Graham? Gordon? Something beginning with 'G'. "His podcast on addiction is my favourite," the PE teacher said to Rav. "He says it's not the substance that's the problem, but our compulsive thinking. He has a way of cutting through the crap." Mark hadn't a clue who they were talking about. He toyed with trying to join in, but couldn't think what to say. He'd have to walk over to them, or move to another chair. Anyway, Katie was the one he wanted to connect with – and she hadn't even turned up. This always happens, he thought. What's the point in coming to these events when no one's interested in getting to know me.

"Brothers and sisters," said Eric. The 'focalizer', he called himself. "Let us begin with some silence. Allow the choppy waters on the surface of your mind to become still." He spoke in slow motion.

Mark tried to get comfortable in the wooden-seated chair. If he did come back next week, he'd get here earlier and bag one of the comfier ones.

"Now, let your eyelids close... Relax your shoulders... Rest your hands in your lap..." Eric's words were a lullaby. "Feel the sensation of the carpet under your feet."

Almost in unison, half the group uncrossed their legs.

"Become aware of your breath. Breathe in... And breathe out... In... And out... Notice the still point at the end of your out-breath. There is nothing you need do. Allow yourself simply to be."

A car drove by. Mark could hear the wind gusting. The BBC weather site had warned of gales. He had to remember not to put the rubbish bin out, or the wind would blow it over in the night. He caught his mind wandering and focussed once more on his breath. He'd read somewhere that it's healthier to draw breath from your stomach, rather than your chest. He tried it. Deep breath in... His stomach gave a loud whine. Immediately, he clenched it and returned to his normal shallow breaths.

A dog barked next door. Mark's stomach churned again. He wanted the silence to be over. He could meditate equally well at home. £50 he'd paid to take part in these workshops. He might have been better off spending the money on books. At least it was going to charity.

The doorbell chime made him start. Katie? No, it'd be that dreadlocked hippy who fancied himself as the joker of the group – he'd been late last week too.

Eric crossed the room. "If your thoughts stray," he said as he passed by Mark, "bring them back to your breath".

Mark listened to the sound of the door being opened. He heard Eric's warm "Namaste".

Then, Katie's soprano voice: "Sorry I'm late. I've had a hell of a day."

"I'm so glad you made it. Let me take your coat."

Mark imagined her perching on the bottom stair to slip off her shoes.

"...And your worries," Eric said. "You don't need to carry them with you. Will you do something for me? For the next two hours, will you let them go?"

Katie took the free chair next to Mark and, with his eyes still closed, he inhaled the scent of her perfume. The same one she'd worn last week, understated and sweet.

His tummy burbled again.

* * *

From his chair, Eric made eye contact with everyone in turn. When he met Mark's eyes, Mark nodded back, but Eric continued to gaze at him. Much longer and he would have had to look away.

"Welcome, brothers and sisters," Eric said finally. "We gather together. We gather as one." He paused. "'*Your task is not to seek for love, but merely to seek and find all the barriers within yourself that you have built against it.*' [20] That's from Chapter 16 of the Text."

Daisy raised her hand. "I love that quote. But isn't it from Rumi?" When Eric didn't respond, she turned to her neighbour. "I'm sure it is. A friend wrote it in a card she sent me, and when I asked her, she said it came from Rumi. She'd checked on the internet."

"You may be right," said Eric. He sipped from his tumbler. "Rumi or *A Course in Miracles*, the channel isn't important when the ultimate source is the same. Listen again: '*Your task is not to seek for love, but merely to seek and* *find all the barriers within yourself that you have built against it. It is not necessary to seek for what is true, but it is necessary to seek for what is false.'*²¹ Those barriers we build stop us expressing love. And they keep us from experiencing it too. Without them, joy and peace would be ours."

"Why do we build those barriers?" Daisy asked.

Eric gazed at her, waiting, perhaps, for her to draw her own answer from a place deep within.

"...There's something inside us. Inside me, I should say. A voice, I suppose. It wants to be right. Or at least to be acknowledged. Like when you shared that quote just now. I know it's from Rumi. It shouldn't matter, but to me it does."

"To you? Or to that voice?"

Daisy nodded. "The voice."

"*A Course in Miracles* calls that the ego. We might say it's our self with a small 's'. It's the part of us which wants to be special. To stand apart from the Whole." He paused before continuing. "Do you want to be right, or to be happy? The small self would rather be right. I will only choose happiness – which means choosing peace of mind – if I listen to a different Voice."

Eric reached for his well-worn copy of the Course, brown parcel tape holding it together at the spine. "Even this can be a barrier," he said, lifting up the book. "If we intellectualise it. If we spend time arguing over interpretations or insist it's the only way... So for today I want to keep it simple and focus on a basic question. What keeps you from experiencing joy and peace as your constant state?" He fell silent, inviting peoples' thoughts.

"Forgetfulness," Rav said. "I forget I'm not my ego."

"Say more. What happens to you when you forget?"

Mark liked Rav. He didn't say much, but when he did, he hit the spot.

"I become anxious," said Rav. "When I forget who I am, fear comes in."

"Fear is at the heart of all our defences," said Eric.

"When we feel fearful, our reaction is to protect ourselves. But remember, God didn't create anything to be fearful of! In the Introduction to the Course, we read: *'The opposite of love is fear, but what is all-encompassing can have no opposite.'* [22] In the holy instant when we become aware of our Identity and return to love, fear dissolves. We reclaim the peace of God."

After a short silence, Eric addressed them again. "I'm going to invite you to reflect on the barriers you've built against love. How shall we do this? Let's work in threes."

Mark looked to his left and right. If Eric split the room down the middle, he'd be in a different group to Katie.

"Rav, why don't you work with Irene and Daisy? Geoff and Katie and Mark, will you work together?"

Mark held back a smile.

"I've some cards for you to use as prompts." Eric handed a set to Geoff, another to Daisy. "On them, I've written different blocks to love. For example, there's anger and fear. I'd like you each to select one that you struggle with. We experience all of them at different times, but for this evening, please pick one to explore."

Geoff flicked through the cards, each a different colour. Mark couldn't read them from where he sat.

"When you've settled on one, I invite you to share with the other people in your group how it blocks your awareness of love's presence. Be as honest and as open as you can. This is a safe space – remember the ground rules we've all agreed. Most of the time we won't be conscious of our ego's defence mechanisms, so we need to bring them to the Light. The two people who are listening, your role is to be that Light for your brother; to offer only love. So Rav, Irene – when Daisy is sharing, uphold her, but resist the temptation to comment or give advice. It's a chance to extend miracles to one another. To listen and be listened to; to see and to be seen."

"How long should we speak for?" asked Daisy.

"Take up to fifteen minutes. Then move on to the next person so you each get a turn to share. The purpose here is *'to seek for what is false'*.[23] The Course refers to the ego's defences as calls for love. But what you really are *needs* no defending. So the next time your protections are triggered, be aware of what's going on within you. Then you can make a conscious decision to choose peace instead. Once you're ready, your Inner Guide will show you how."

* * *

"Shall we go to the other room?" Katie suggested. "I find it hard to concentrate when other people are speaking nearby."

Geoff beat Mark to it. "Good idea."

Mark let Katie lead the way. She wore an orange-red mini dress over skinny jeans. The colour complemented her hair. He knew he should see no one as a body, but he couldn't help that he found her cute.

"Ooh… It's dark in here." She turned the light off and on again. Two of the bulbs in the chandelier were spent.

Geoff pulled back a chair from the coffee table for Katie to sit down. "How's your week been?"

"Manic," she said. "I almost didn't make it tonight, but I'm glad I did. This stillness and reflection time is exactly what I needed. How about you?"

"I'm muddling by," said Geoff. "I hope you got a chance to unwind at the weekend?"

Once again, Mark found himself on the margins of a conversation.

"Well, I took the dog for a walk on the heath on Sunday morning before it rained." Katie turned to Mark. "How was your weekend? It *is* Mark, isn't it?"

"Um, good, thanks… What kind of dog do you have?"

"A labradoodle named Max. He keeps me on my toes."

"So…" Geoff coughed without covering his mouth. Mark shrunk back, away from the germs. "We've got these cards."

"Oh yes, sorry," said Katie. "Would you read them out?"

"Okay, here goes… Fear. Guilt. Busyness. Anger." Geoff lingered a moment on the red card. "Appropriate colour for that one. Pride. Oh, he's spelled this one wrong: *Judgement'* shouldn't have an 'e'."

"Who wants to go first?" asked Mark.

The others glanced at each other, then at him. "Why don't you kick us off?" said Geoff.

Mark couldn't very well say no. He accepted the cards and shuffled through the deck. He could speak all night about judgment. He certainly did enough of it. Everyone judges, surely. But if he spoke about how he judged people, he'd come across like a snake to Katie. He'd rather someone else went first, so he could gauge how much of himself to reveal. He'd play it safe. Katie had mentioned her week being manic. Maybe he could offer some tips. "I'm choosing busyness," he began, resting the green-coloured card on his leg.

"Whenever you're ready," said Geoff.

Mark noticed his pulse had quickened. He always got nervous around women he liked. "I used to struggle with busyness. A few years ago, I had a demanding job. When you're a fast-streamer in the civil service, they put you in challenging roles. It was constant pressure; never any let up in the pace.

"I live out of town, so the commuting added to my stress. I'd get home shattered. When I still had a TV, I'd flop on the sofa and that would be my evening. Hardly a life. At weekends I'd be drained, and I'd take my frustration out on whoever I was with. I'd snap at the silliest things. I'd completely lost touch with what's important."

"You felt overburdened," Katie said.

"That's a good way of putting it. Always rushing to finish a task, so I could move on to the next. Or planning how I'd tackle my inbox the following day. I'd be juggling a hundred things, but not be fully present with any of them."

"Have you tried mindfulness?" she asked.

"You're getting ahead of me. About seven years ago, I came across *A Course in Miracles*. I started doing the lessons – I got about as far as Lesson 50, but I couldn't keep up with them. At the end of a busy day, I didn't want to think. So, instead of watching TV, I made a point of having quiet time before bed. A ritual, you could call it. I'd say to myself, 'right, it's 9 o'clock; no more screens or looking at my phone'."

"Did it help?"

"Definitely. I noticed that, if I skipped my quiet time for a couple of days, my stress levels soared.

"At work, everyone wanted to make an impression. It became an arms race to stay in the office the latest, and take on most tasks. I figured, if I could get promoted, I could pay off my mortgage sooner and *then* I'd be able to slow down. But, the more I made space to listen to my Guide, the more I realised… That way of living wasn't making me happy. And it wasn't helping my relationships either. It's like Bill Thetford said to Helen Schucman before she began receiving the Course: there had to be another way."

"So you listened to your Inner Guide?" asked Katie.

Mark thought about it. "Yes, by making space for it to be heard. The Course teaches that whatever we experience, we're doing it to ourselves. No one was *making* me stressed, or *forcing* me to work fifty-hour weeks. I took two weeks off, my longest break since I'd started in the job. I didn't go away anywhere, but used the time to reflect on what I wanted to do with my life. And more importantly, on the kind of person I wanted to be. I'd sit with a question… 'How can I be more loving? How can I be more patient?' And then I waited to see what emerged."

"Did you get any guidance?" she asked.

"Nothing specific, as in 'do this' or 'do that'. But I did get a sense of what really mattered to me, and what would count as important at the end of my life. I realised I'd been playing a role and had lost touch with my real Self."

Katie and Geoff leaned forward, properly listening, he could tell.

"Then, after a month back at work, a post came up in another team. It wasn't a fast-stream role, but I felt right away that I'd enjoy it. I applied and the interview went perfectly. Before they told me the results, I knew I'd got the job. Even better, they'd advertised it as open to part-time working, so I asked my new boss if I could switch to a four-day week. Reducing my hours is one of the best decisions I've made. It's given me the space to re-centre myself, which has made a real difference in my relationships… When I'm with someone, I can give them my full attention – and I'm less likely to fly off the handle when my train gets cancelled because of the wrong kind of leaves on the line! I'm healthier too. Since I went part-time, I've not had a single day off sick."

"I'd love to work part-time," said Katie. "But I couldn't afford to."

"Well, I need to be more careful with money," Mark replied. "I don't go abroad every year, and I don't eat out as often. But I'm relaxed. I'm happier. I've time to do the things I want. Last month I signed up for a photography class. And I'm studying the Course again too, and engaging with it in a deeper way. I wouldn't go back to full-time hours."

"Can I ask a question?" Geoff said.

"Sure."

"Isn't it about balance? I thrive on being busy. I love my job. Well, most of the time! I remember the few months after I'd finished university and before I decided what I wanted to do. My mates were all working, or travelling abroad. With no job back then, I had loads of free time, but I quickly became depressed. I need to be active, to feel like I'm doing something worthwhile. 'Work hard, play hard' suits me best."

"I don't think we're meant to comment?" Katie reminded him. "Sorry, it's my fault for interrupting. Mark, is there anything else you want to say?"

He shook his head. He wasn't sure what he'd expected, but he'd hoped they'd be more positive. Geoff's remarks had left him feeling flat.

"Thank you for sharing with us," she said.

"Yeah, thanks," said Geoff. "Katie, do you want to go next."

"Would you mind going next? I find these things difficult."

Mark put busyness back in the pack and handed the cards to Geoff.

"Okay. Let's tackle judgment. I realise I judge people more than I should. I sometimes catch myself judging kids at school, or their parents mainly, for feeding them junk food and letting them get so unhealthy. At least twenty percent of the kids in my classes can't run one lap of a rugby field without getting out of breath. We're talking about boys of twelve and thirteen! I've got three kids in my year eight class who are medically obese!

"My question would be, when is it okay to judge? Which of my judgments are reasonable, and which ones are unfair?" He spoke to Katie, rarely glancing at Mark. "It's not practical to get away from judging entirely. Thinking about it, there are some things that I can't accept; that are not okay, by anyone's standard. If a war's broken out and women and children are bombed in their homes, or people are being tortured – I can't not judge that. I don't want to be like some people I've met in groups like this who go around saying, 'It doesn't matter, because it's only a dream'. I don't know the Course as well as other people here, but it talks about forgiveness, right? What I try to do is notice when a judgment comes up. And then forgive myself for having the judgmental thought. I'm a work in progress, that's for sure!"

"We all are!" Katie said. "In terms of your question, Geoff, I think ideally we'd let the Holy Spirit judge *all* things for us. The problem with attempting to judge for ourselves is that we can't see the full picture. We don't know what past experiences might have led another person to behave a certain way: how they were brought up; how their own parents may have been wounded. But there's another problem with judgment," she added. "It doesn't bring us peace."

"And when we're not at peace, we won't be happy," Mark offered.

Katie smiled at him, then spoke again to Geoff. "I appreciate it's difficult to see that with wars and terrorist attacks and everything else going on. But we can maybe start with people closer to home, like those children in your PE class? And whatever we think about them, being kind."

"I try," said Geoff. "I should probably try harder."

"A thought came to me in one of my quiet times," Mark said. "A prayer, really. When I have an unkind thought about someone, or when I'm tempted to judge them, let me say in my mind, 'I am in God and God is in me. Love is my essence, my truth and my being.' Then, let me say, as I think of the other person, 'You are in God and God is in you. Love is your essence, your truth and your being'."

"That's beautiful," said Katie. "What unites us is greater than the differences. If only I'd remember that.

Geoff, we interrupted you. Do you want to say any more?"

"I'm done," he said. "I'd like to hear from you. What's your biggest block?"

"Crumbs," Katie said. "You're both so eloquent. I don't know how I can follow that."

"That's already a judgment!" Geoff pointed out. "Comparing yourself with others."

"Give me a moment. Which of these to choose?... No, I know which one I need to face up to. I knew as soon as I saw it. That one." She pointed to the card saying guilt. "This whole book is about forgiveness, but I still don't get it. I've had to give up reading the paper because it makes me so angry, or depressed. Did you hear about the boy who threw acid in the face of a thirteen-year-old girl? He disfigured her, permanently ruined her life. I felt pure hatred for that boy. I wanted to throw acid in *his* face so he'd know how it felt.

"And then I pick up the Course, trying to make sense of this world – and obviously I can't, because the whole point is, it *doesn't* make sense. And I realise, those people in the papers – the perpetrators – they're like me. I may not have done all those things, but I've *thought about* doing a lot of them. Maybe not exactly the same, but close enough…" She stopped. "I could use a drink."

"Shall I get you some water from the other room?" Mark asked.

"No, I meant something stronger than water. I don't suppose Eric has any gin?"

"There's a big difference though, between thinking something and doing it?" said Geoff. "To me, there is."

"I always had to live up to my parents' expectations," Katie continued. "Whatever I achieved, they wanted more. My dad's a football manager… I guess he treated me like a player in his team."

"Would I have heard of him?" asked Geoff.

"My dad? You might if you follow football, but he

never managed in the Premier League. He did well at his first club and they won promotion. Before long, a bigger club offered him a job, which meant we had to move north. But things didn't work out for him there and after a few months they sacked him, so we moved again. As soon as I made any friends – which didn't come easily – we upped sticks. I was always the new girl, having to fit in.

"When I was fourteen – I'd just started seeing my first boyfriend – dad says to me and my sister, 'right, girls, we're moving to London'. So, after autumn half term, I'm starting at another new school where I don't know anyone and face another battle to make friends. One girl, Misha, saw me with my dad and recognized him. That's the only reason she let me into her clique." She looked at each of them. "I've not spoken about this to anyone before."

"You don't have to say more if you don't want to," said Geoff.

"No, I need to. Because, otherwise, you won't understand what I'm talking about: how can I forgive myself after this?"

"What you share, stays between the three of us. Right, Mark?"

"Totally."

"Misha could be bitchy if she turned against you. A bully, basically. I guess she has her own story. I don't know what her parents were like. She'd put anyone down to make herself look bigger. One girl in our class, Anne, didn't have many friends. She struggled with her weight, which made her an easy target for Misha. I remember sitting in class one day when the teacher was late. Misha began ripping pages from my notebook and scrunching them into balls to chuck at Anne. When they hit her, people laughed, but I didn't find it funny. Then Misha shoves me with her elbow. 'Your turn, Katie. You throw one.' I didn't want to, but I couldn't stand up to her."

"We all do things like that when we're kids and don't know better," said Geoff. "I've seen far worse at the school where I work."

"You were fourteen," Mark added. "You shouldn't feel guilty about it now."

Katie sighed. "If that were it! One Monday morning we're waiting for registration and Anne walks in. She's had her hair done up, a bit like Misha's. It looks really nice. But Misha sidles up to her, saying, 'Ooh… look at Plump Arse with her new perm. You out to impress Craig?' Everybody in our year had the hots for Craig. I went up to Anne too. No one made me do it this time. And do you know what I said to her? '…You'll never be pretty, Anne. No boy will ever go out with you, so what's the point in trying?'" Katie cupped a hand over her mouth.

"Okay, so that's a mean thing to say, but you were fourteen for goodness' sake. We all make mistakes."

"She killed herself, Geoff. One week later. She swallowed her gran's sleeping tablets."

Mark was stunned. As the silence drew out longer, he wanted to say something. But no words came.

Geoff said what he was thinking: "Can I give you a hug?"

Katie nodded, but after a moment, she pulled away from him and went to the window. "Now do you see?" she said, staring into the darkness. "If anyone can still like me, knowing what I've done, it repels me from them. Because, basically, I killed her. And if they're not appalled by that, there's something wrong with *them*. That's how I feel. That's my block. And I'm supposed to forgive myself? Tell me how?"

Mark realised that anything he said would sound like a platitude. He knew God didn't condemn her, but also that it wouldn't help if he told her that now. Then it came to him – a line from the Course: *'Forgiveness… does nothing… It merely looks, and waits, and judges not.'* [24] He wasn't meant to *say* anything, merely to see her as Christ would; innocent, as God created her. Until she could see the truth about herself, he'd look and wait and judge her not.

4

Irene

Eric stood behind his chair, resting his arms on its back. He looked rather pale, thought Irene. She noticed he hadn't shaved.

"Before we start," he said, "Daisy sends her apologies. She has a migraine, so won't be joining us tonight."

Irene felt a tightening in her chest. She would have expected Daisy to call her to let her know she wasn't coming.

She glanced around the room, conscious of being the only woman there.

"Has anyone heard from Katie?" asked Geoff.

Katie had left early last week. Irene had assumed she'd been feeling unwell.

"She's not been in touch with me," said Eric. "We'll start without her and see if she comes. I'd like you all to join me in the other room."

Please, not another group-sharing activity, thought Irene as she hauled herself up from her seat. She didn't mind opening up to Daisy, but felt uneasy among the men. She followed the others into a dim room with a dining table. The chandelier had five lamps, but only two were lit. Vanilla air-freshener couldn't mask the stale odour of damp.

The men had gathered round Eric in an arc. She peered between the shoulders of Rav and Geoff, who moved to give her more space.

Their host had his laptop open on the table. Behind the computer stood a brass candelabrum with red candlesticks. Eric struck a match, but its flame died before he could light the first candle. It took him two more matches to kindle all three.

Irene watched with the others, not knowing what to think.

With the candles lit, he turned his attention to the computer. He pressed something and a picture appeared on the screen – a golden bull with a disk on its head.

"Meet El Toro Grande," Eric said, louder than he usually spoke. Theatrically, with one hand on his paunch, he bowed before the image of the bull.

"Is this for real?" Irene heard someone mutter.

"Will you join me, Christopher?" Eric asked, turning round. "Mark? Irene?"

Irene didn't move, but waited for a cue from someone else. He couldn't seriously expect her to bow to an *idol*?

Geoff was frowning. Mark looked perplexed. Only Rav had a smile on his face.

"What's the matter?" Eric protested. "Will no one worship my bull? Wait!" he said. "Perhaps something else?" He pressed a key on his computer and the screen changed. Now it showed a sports car. Eric bowed again, then met Irene's eyes. "You *still* won't join me? But it's an Aston Martin! My, you lot really are a hard bunch to please. What about this one?" The picture changed to a couple holding hands on a beach, watching a spectacular sunset.

Rav was on the brink of laughter.

"I get it!" said Mark. "I see what you're doing."

Irene had no idea.

The pictures on the screen kept changing: a bottle of

wine; a trophy with blue ribbons tied to its handles; a thatched-roof cottage, wisteria climbing its walls. A mother with a baby in her arms. And then a copy of *A Course in Miracles*. Eric bowed yet again, twice this time. "What's so funny, Rav? Have I lost my marbles?"

"You're showing us ourselves," said Rav. "The bull represents an idol, but the other pictures are idols too. They're some of the things we worship."

"They're some of the things *I've* worshipped," said Eric. "At various points in my life. Well, maybe not the bull – though he *would* look fetching on my mantelpiece, don't you think?"

"You had us worried," said Christopher. "With your graven images, we thought you'd gone over to the dark side."

"Not yet," said Eric. "But it's only twenty past seven. The night is young."

* * *

Irene wasn't sure about Eric's performance. She wondered what Daisy would have made of it. The sports car she could understand – he had a point that people worship money, or the objects money can buy. But how could he compare that with a mother holding her newborn baby? He'd gone too far.

When they returned to the sitting room, Geoff approached Eric. "Can I ask a question?"

Irene loitered where she could listen in.

"If you go into a church – a Catholic one, or Eastern Orthodox – there are lots of icons. But no one calls them idols. What's the difference? When does an icon become an idol?"

"How would *you* answer that question, Geoff, if someone asked you?"

"Hmmm..."

"Take a moment. Listen within," Eric encouraged.

"People don't worship icons. They can help us to get in touch with God, but we don't make them into gods. They point beyond themselves."

"You see, you did know after all. Right, is everyone back in the room? Who are we missing? Ah, Rav, here he comes..."

When they'd all returned to their seats, Eric addressed the group. "An idol is not only a graven image. It's anything that takes God's place in our hearts and minds; anything that distracts us from awareness of our true identity.

"We say we have no other gods before Him, but how do we spend most of our time? ... What goal are we pursuing? ... Is it peace? ... Whenever we notice that we are not at peace it's an indication that we've identified as a separate self. That mean's we've chosen a different 'god'." Eric reached for his copy of the Course. He took a deep, audible breath. "I'd like to focus on Lesson 34."

Irene stretched for her bag and realised to her horror that she'd forgotten her book.

"It's okay," Eric said to her. "We'll be doing this as a meditation. Paragraphs three and four of Lesson 34, 'I could see peace instead of this':

> *'...Search your mind for fear thoughts, anxiety-provoking situations, "offending" personalities or events, or anything else about which you are harbouring unloving thoughts. Note them all casually, repeating the idea slowly as you watch them arise in your mind, and let each one go, to be replaced by the next.*[25]
>
> *'I could see peace instead of this.*
>
> *'If you begin to experience difficulty in thinking of specific subjects, continue to*

repeat the idea to yourself in an unhurried manner, without applying it to anything in particular. Be sure, however, not to make any specific exclusions.'" [26]

Eric laid his book on the table and sat with his palms facing upwards on his lap. "This practice works best with your eyes closed. Search your mind for anything that's disturbing you and simply tell yourself, 'I could see peace instead of this'."

Irene saw the others relax their posture as they followed his invitation to be still. With some reluctance, she shut her eyes.

'I could see peace instead of this,' she repeated. Instead of what? What was making her uneasy? It nagged her that Daisy hadn't called her to say she felt unwell and would miss tonight's session. She felt hurt that she'd contacted Eric instead. For a second, Irene wondered if perhaps Daisy had mislaid her phone number. But it would be on Daisy's mobile, as that time she couldn't make yoga class, she'd rang to let Daisy know. Thinking about it, she'd never had a call or even a text from Daisy. Maybe Daisy didn't think of her as a friend.

'I could see peace instead of this.'

Her son never called her either. She missed not having him around. She knew he had his own life with his studies and his friends, but when he did occasionally answer her calls, he'd cut her short after a minute or two: 'Mum, I'm really busy...' or 'Mum, I've got to go.'

'I could see peace instead of this.'

Her ex, and that thirty-something floozy he'd taken up with, Deborah, the *Eurostar* trolley dolly. She didn't know what riled her more – John leaving, or him still being with Deborah eight years later. She'd been certain it was his mid-life crisis, a fling that wouldn't last.

'I could see peace instead of this.'

Eric's show this evening, when he'd bowed down to idols and then trivialized a mother's love by lumping it in the same category as selfish desires. Probably he didn't have children of his own, because if he did he'd know the difference – and how much she'd sacrificed to bring up a child without expecting anything in return.

Her sister, for being mum's favourite.

Her mum, for having a favourite – and it not being her.

Daisy, again, for being so sleek and confident.

Herself, for being clumsy and shy. And for not being able to hang on to the love of her life.

Goodness, thought Irene. So many resentments beneath the surface. She'd opened a Pandora's box.

She repeated the idea: 'I could see peace instead of this'.

* * *

Eric struck his singing bowl and brought Irene back from her reverie. "Would anyone like to share what came up for them?" he asked, once the echo had faded into silence.

"I don't mind going first if no one else wants to," said Christopher. "I went to put my rubbish out last night and found my dustbin filled with someone else's trash."

"How did that make you feel?" asked Eric.

"I swore out loud. They'd stuffed it full of cardboard. There's a recycling bin for that. I ended up having to take it all out and put it in my own green bin. If I'd known whose it was, I'd have stuck it in theirs – but there are four flats, so it could have been anyone's."

"How do you feel?" Eric asked again.

"I've told you. When I went inside, I slammed the door. They've got their own bin, so why the hell use mine?"

"Do you think they did it deliberately?"

"There's a sign on the lid saying 'Flat C'. They could hardly have missed it."

"Could there be another reason why someone put the rubbish in your bin, other than it being an attack on you?"

"I suppose theirs could've been full, but in that case they should've waited 'til the next collection, or asked me first if they wanted to use mine."

"I sense that you're not at peace about the situation."

"It's their attitude of not considering others that makes me mad."

"Is it their attitude that makes you angry, or is it the story that you've attached to the situation? Let's say the person had been blind, and unable to see the sign on your bin? Would you feel the same way then?"

"No, but I know who lives in the other flats and none of them is blind."

"If I offered you a choice: an apology from the culprit and a guarantee they'll never put rubbish in your bin again – or a feeling of peace so complete, so all-encompassing, that no matter what happened, it would never be disturbed… Which would you go for?"

"I'm not sure," said Christopher. "Probably the apology!"

Geoff and Mark both laughed.

"The truth is," said Eric, "no one can offer guarantees in this world. There will always be things beyond our control. But we *can* choose peace in any moment… I'm being hard on you, but actually you're doing well. You've already taken the first step – which is to recognise that you're not at peace. And the reason you're not is that you've made up your own mind about the situation and what it means. You've perceived it as an attack."

"An attack?"

"Anger is a defence-mechanism, a knee-jerk response

when we perceive a challenge or a threat."

"I hadn't thought of it like that. I guess I do see it as a challenge."

"If something happens that we perceive as a threat to our sense of self – whether to our body or our beliefs – our automatic response is self-defence. We fight or we flee like animals when they spot a predator. We mightn't physically fight or run away, but our emotional responses kick in – anger; fear. And sometimes we need that: if we step into a road and a car's speeding towards us, we want that triggered response.

"But often the threat is imagined. Well, ultimately, you could say it's *all* made up, but let's keep things at a more basic level for now. There's no threat to your safety when you find a neighbour's rubbish in your bin. The threat is to your self-hood – to your personal boundaries or ideas about what's right."

"I get what you're saying," said Christopher. "I don't *choose* to be angry. But in the heat of the moment I react."

"It's not a conscious choice. If we believe we're separate individuals; if we see ourselves as existing in a body that we know is going to die, it's inevitable that we'll feel vulnerable. These fears are at an unconscious level. We've buried them, but they're there. When we react with anger, it's a symptom of our fear.

"It takes practice. You notice now the feelings you have about the neighbour and the bin. Maybe next time it happens, you'll catch yourself sooner. Once you become aware of your thoughts in relation to a situation, you can notice whether they're making you happy or whether they're blocking your peace. You can then decide if hanging on to them is helpful, or if you want to let them go."

"How do we let them go?" asked Geoff.

"By asking for help. Say, 'I could choose peace instead of this. I am willing to see this differently.' That little willingness is all it takes. Once you listen to the Voice for God, the Voice which recalls you to your true Self, you know there's nothing to fear. If what you really are isn't affected by the situation; if you can't be harmed, there's no need to be angry, or upset. It doesn't matter what the outward situation is: rubbish in your dustbin, a row with your loved one, losing your job. Even a terminal diagnosis. *'Nothing real can be threatened.'* [27] You know that what *can* be threatened was never real, but simply a picture you made up. *'Therein lies the peace of God.'*"[28]

Irene wondered, again, if she was the only one who didn't understand. *Notice how you're feeling.* Okay, she got that. *Decide if you want to hang on to those feelings.* Well, of course she didn't *want* to be upset. But after that, he'd lost her. She glanced at the others. Rav's perpetual smile had broadened into a grin.

"Would anyone else like to share what forgiveness opportunities came up for them in the meditation?" Eric asked.

"Mine's simple," said Geoff. "Donald Trump."

"How do you feel about your brother Donald?"

"They've given the biggest job in the world to the man with the biggest ego. He's convinced he's right about everything and anyone who thinks differently is an ass. But what gets me even more is all those people who voted for him. What does that say about the world?"

"Focus on your feelings. How do you feel when Donald Trump is on the news and he says something you disagree with?"

"Irritated. Angry."

"Do you like those feelings? Are you willing to let them go?"

Geoff paused. "If I'm honest, I *do* like feeling angry about Trump."

"Say more…"

"I suppose he's a scapegoat. We all like a villain. If I

see him as guilty, I feel better about myself."

"The Course calls it projection," said Eric. "Again, this is all going on unconsciously. We've a deep-seated guilt because we think we've cut ourselves off from God. We haven't, but all the evidence we see in this world tells us separation is real. When we project that guilt onto others, it diverts attention from our own guilt.

"And it's okay if you're not ready yet to let those feelings go. The first step is simply to *recognise* the feelings – anger, worry, sadness, depression – and the thoughts behind them. And to acknowledge that if you wanted to, you *could* choose peace instead.

"You're not persuaded? Is God withholding peace from us? And if God isn't, then who is? Donald Trump? If we think that, we're giving him power over our own happiness. He's not simply the President, he's become the ruler of our mind."

"Can I say something?" Mark asked. "Could it be that the more we resist Donald Trump, the more we fuel his fire? If, instead of fighting him, we saw him as crying out for love – like a lost child – then maybe he'd feel less need to defend himself and his way of seeing the world?"

"That's possible," said Eric. "Or perhaps there'd be no outward change in the way he acts – but either way it wouldn't affect our peace. … Irene, would you like to share what came up for you?"

She jumped when Eric said her name. "Um… I had Donald Trump as well." She heard a ripple of laughter.

"Only him?" pressed Eric. "If he's the only one who upsets your peace, that's pretty good going."

Irene felt a quivering inside her… Something she had to say. "When we were in the other room and you showed us those pictures of different idols…"

"Go on."

"Why did you include one of a mother holding her baby? What's wrong with a mother's love?"

"Irene, I'm sorry." Eric looked at her with soft eyes. "I should have explained it more clearly. The love of a parent for their child is one of the purest, most selfless, forms of love on earth. I can say with all honesty that I love my daughter as if she were part of me. Though there have been times when she was younger and going through her wild phase when I've felt a whole range of other emotions too.

"But the love I feel for her is what the Course calls 'special love'. Let me speak from my own experience. When my wife gave birth and I saw Emma for the first time, it was love at first sight – yet until that moment, I'd thought babies were noisy, pooping, burping things and I wanted as little to do with them as possible. I still feel that way when it comes to other peoples' babies.

"When Emma was at school and they put on a play, I went to see her. I had no interest in the other children or how they played their roles. I dare say it will have been the same for the other parents. A parent's love is specific. It's love for one child, for *their* child... It's beautiful. It can give us a worldly experience of selfless love. But it's only a faint intimation of the Love that was given us to share.

"Christ's Love sees no difference between my child and your child. It pours out equally on everyone. It's unconditional. It doesn't ask anything back, or change with circumstances or time. It overlooks separation. Lover and beloved are one.

"Until we use Christ's vision, we're rooted in the world of forms. We're focussed on the frame, and overlooking the painting. We're keeping ourselves from heaven."

* * *

After the closing meditation, Irene said a quick goodbye to everyone. She slipped out of the room, but as she sat to put on her shoes, Eric joined her in the hall. He retrieved her coat from among the others and helped her into it. "I've a feeling that my answer earlier didn't really help you," he said.

"It's not that," she said. "It's just... I'm not sure if *A Course in Miracles* is for me."

"Don't try to force it. There are as many ways home as there are people. Our task is simply to step back and allow ourselves to be led by the Inner Guide who recalls our mind to peace."

"I want to believe that God loves everyone, but how can I, when I see all the misery in the world? People suffer. I've worked as a nurse. One patient might recover, but the person in the next bed dies. And it doesn't matter how kind they've been, or what religion they are, or if their family are by their bedside praying and begging for them to get better. Sometimes they don't."

"May I give you a hug?"

Irene nodded. The first couple of sessions, when everyone had exchanged hugs at the end, she'd felt uneasy. Now, though, she'd become used to this closing ritual. Still she tensed a little as Eric held her in a squeeze.

"This world *is* unfair," he said, letting go and stepping back. "Illness. Pain. Loss of a loved one. But if you accept what *A Course in Miracles* is saying, none of that is down to God. I used to struggle with the Course's theology too – it's a very radical teaching, so different to the belief system most of us have been brought up with. But the more I considered it; the more I sat in stillness and asked for guidance, the more it began to make sense.

"*'God did not create a meaningless world'*, it says in one of the lessons.[29] The world can appear to be a meaningless place. We're born; we grow up. We experience some highs, but none of them last forever. Sooner or later, we have to let go of everything – until our bodies grow weak and stop working too. And that's if we're lucky. Many people die young, or without ever knowing happiness. If that were it – if that were the ultimate truth – then God would have a lot to answer for: creating us as bodies, watching us suffer awhile, and finally letting us die.

"But Love wouldn't do that, and I trust in God's Love – despite what my senses perceive. Recall the quote I shared in our first session: *'Nothing real can be threatened. Nothing unreal exists.'* [30] Suffering comes from our false beliefs about what we are. Our dreams might be pleasant, or they might be nightmares. But one way or the other, they're merely dreams."

Irene looked over her shoulder as Rav and Christopher came into the hallway.

"There I go again," said Eric. "Trying to find words, when there are none, really, to describe what I want to share. It's not important which particular path we follow. What matters is to let ourselves be guided by Love." He opened the front door for her and the bitter November air burst into the hall.

"Back to reality," said Christopher, zipping up his jacket.

"Back to the dream," said Rav.

5

Rav

As the silence continued, Rav sank deeper into meditation. When he became aware of sensations – an itch above his ankle, the ticking of someone's wristwatch – he acknowledged them... then immediately let them go. After some time, he sensed one or two of the other people in the room becoming unsettled. The opening period of quiet was going on for longer than it had in the previous sessions. He heard someone shift in their seat. A woman sighed. A little while later, she cleared her throat. Then coughed.

Rav noticed himself becoming uneasy. Not with the extended quiet, but with other peoples' resistance to it. He wondered for how much longer Eric would continue to hold the silence. A little resistance can be sat with and worked through. But in a gathering where people are becoming restless, where they aren't used to meditation, it may be better to end.

He caught his mind taking over and its subtle judgments of peoples' impatience. Letting those thoughts go, he directed attention to the room, appealing to the *Atman* – the true Self – of everyone present.

The restless sounds subsided, or maybe he became less conscious of them.

After a few minutes, Eric spoke to end the silence, repeating the line he'd used at the start: "*'In quiet I receive God's word today'*"[31]

When Rav opened his eyes, he saw from the clock that half an hour had passed since they'd begun.

"What a wonderful meditation. Thank you," said Irene. "I feel so calm."

"It went on longer than last week's," said Daisy.

"We were beginning to wonder…" Christopher said to Eric, "…if you'd fallen asleep!"

Eric smiled, a little uneasily, Rav thought.

"This evening," Eric began, "we'll be exploring guidance and decision-making. The Course tells us that God's Voice speaks to us all through the day. But to hear that Voice we need to still the chatter in our minds. A meditation practice can help.

"When I first began to meditate, a part of me insisted there were a hundred and one other things I could more usefully be doing with the time. But when, despite my ego's protestations, I committed to a regular practice, I saw the effects it had on my state of mind. I felt more peaceful, more centred… Over time, it became easier to carry that peace with me throughout the day.

"We try to navigate our own way through life, making decisions based on what we think would maximise the pleasure we experience and minimise the pain. But the Course tells us that we don't perceive our own best interests. If that's true; if we can't see the whole picture of how our choices would affect us – let alone all the other people involved – wouldn't we be better off handing over our decisions to the One Who does?"

Eric read from a card: "*'Say to the Holy Spirit only, "Decide for me," and it is done. For His decisions are reflections of what God knows about you,…'* – 'you' here means your true Self – *'…and in this light, error of any kind becomes impossible. Why would you struggle so frantically to anticipate all you cannot know, when all knowledge lies behind every decision the Holy*

Spirit makes for you?...' [32]

"I'd like us to listen together to a section of the Text called Rules for Decision. It's Part 1 of Chapter 30, if you'd like to follow in your book. By the way, 'Rules' might sound authoritarian, but I understand them as a framework for living – a bit like the Rule of St Benedict which monastic communities adopt. They're for our benefit. When I follow these rules each day, it helps me experience the peace and joy I really want." Eric leaned forward and pressed a button on his portable CD player.

"*Chapter 30. The New Beginning*…" the recording began.

Rav focussed on the narrator's words, following them in his newly-acquired copy of the book.

"Wow," said Daisy, when they reached the end of the section and Eric stopped the CD. "That's a lot to take in."

"Let's take it slowly," said Eric. "We've the rest of the evening to devote to this. The section begins by saying that *'Decisions are continuous,'* and that we don't always know when we're making them.[33] For much of the day we're on automatic pilot. We're not conscious that we're making decisions at all. The question is, Who or what *is* our automatic pilot? The answer goes a long way to shaping the kind of day we'll have."

"Do you mean whether we're being guided by the Holy Spirit or by our ego?" asked Mark.

"In a nutshell, yes. Have a look at paragraph 14…"

Rav turned the page in his book. In his bag on the way here, some of the pages had gotten creased.

Eric read aloud: "'*We said you can begin a happy day with the determination not to make decisions by yourself. This seems to be a real decision in itself. And yet, you* cannot *make decisions by yourself. The only question really is with what you choose to make them.*' [34] So, yes, it's a case of which guide we opt to follow. To put it another way, whenever we decide what to do – or what thoughts to entertain – that decision is determined by our response to a more fundamental question: in that moment, who do we think we are?

"The ego tells us we are a separate individual; that it's a dog-eat-dog world, and we need to put ourselves and our loved ones first to stand a chance. The Holy Spirit is the Voice for God, Who is Love. There's a wonderful Workbook Lesson: *'I am one Self, united with my Creator, at one with every aspect of creation…'* [35] That's what the Holy Spirit would have us realise. If we listen to His guidance, we'll make decisions from a place of love rather than fear."

"That's fine in theory," said Geoff. "But during a busy day isn't it inevitable we'll lose touch with our Higher Self and revert to following our ego?"

"It takes practice," Eric replied. "In paragraph 1, we're advised not to be preoccupied with every step we take. It says, *'The proper set, adopted consciously each time you wake, will put you well ahead'.* [36] I interpret 'the proper set' as being in the right mindset – in a state of right-mindedness, as the Course describes it. Have you heard the expression, 'start as you mean to go on'? This paragraph is underlining the importance of taking quiet time every morning to re-centre ourselves and clarify our intention for the day. We're not asked to write a to-do list. It's more about reminding ourselves what kind of feelings we want to experience: the peace of God; a sense of joy.

"There are plenty of Lessons which can help us set our purpose for the day…" Eric read from a card on which he'd written some notes. "Lesson 190: *'I choose the joy of God instead of pain.'* Lesson 242: *'This day is God's. It is my gift to Him.'* Lesson 243: *'Today I will judge nothing that occurs.'* Lesson 255: *'This day I choose to spend in perfect peace.'* Pick whichever appeals most to you. I like to vary it.

"Once I'm clear about the kind of day I want to have, I find it helps to sit for a few minutes. During that quiet time, thoughts come to me about things that I might do.

Some align with the intention I've set, but I realise that others don't. For example, I may have a thought to mow my lawn, even though I know my neighbour who works night shifts is trying to sleep. If anything would divert me from my main goal, I remind myself… 'This day I choose to spend in perfect peace'.

"The second of the Rules for Decision reinforces the dedication we made at the start of our day. It instructs us, *'Throughout the day, at any time you think of it and have a quiet moment for reflection, tell yourself again the kind of day you want; the feelings you would have, the things you want to happen to you, and the things you would experience, and say: "If I make no decisions by myself, this is the day that will be given me"'*.[37]

"'*No decisions by myself*' means no decisions prompted from my ego; no decisions which stem from or strengthen the belief that I'm separate from God and from my brothers."

"How do we tell the difference between the Holy Spirit and our ego?" asked Daisy. "People hear voices in their head, telling them to do all manner of things. How can we be sure it's genuinely coming from God?"

"How do *you* distinguish between the two voices?" Eric asked her. "What's your experience been?"

"Well I… I think I get it right most of the time. Genuine guidance will lead me to be kind."

"Exactly," said Eric. "In the Course, the Holy Spirit is also known as the 'Voice for God'. If God is Love, then the Voice for God will always prompt us to look on our brothers and sisters with love, with compassion, with kindness. It will never urge us to do anything that adds to suffering, or reinforces the illusion of separation – which would amount to the same thing. Guidance coming from the Holy Spirit would have us join with others and see a common interest. Remember the rule of Love – that giving and receiving are the same.

"What other ways might we distinguish between the Voice for God and our ego?" Eric asked.

"How we feel when we follow the guidance," said Mark.

"Can you elaborate?" encouraged Eric.

"It's not always comfortable to follow the Holy Spirit. Sometimes It leads me to do something that's outside my comfort zone… I might feel resistance. But afterwards, I'm much happier than I would have been if I'd ignored the guidance."

Eric nodded. "The Course tells us that the Holy Spirit's Voice is *'the Call to joy'*.[38] God's will for us is perfect happiness. And the Holy Spirit knows what would help us experience that happiness, so it's in our own interest to allow Him to lead the way." He took a deep breath. "Would someone else like to share any tips?"

"I can usually tell if someone is coming from their ego," Christopher said. "Think of politicians baying at one another across the floor of the House of Commons, or a fundamentalist preacher sermonizing on something. If there's any hint of judgment, you can be sure the ego's involved."

"That's true," said Eric. "Although the ego can be devious – it's not always going to be quite as obvious as in the examples you describe. But yes, the ego loves to find fault and condemn. It thrives on guilt. The Holy Spirit sees only innocence. His judgment will always be, 'Behold the Son of God, who is wholly worthy of love'.

"Also, while the ego wants its way now, the Holy Spirit is patient. We're told: *'The Voice of the Holy Spirit does not command, because It is incapable of arrogance. It does not demand, because It does not seek control. It does not overcome, because It does not attack. It merely reminds. … The Voice for God is always quiet, because It speaks of peace.'*[39] What makes it compelling is the truth of its message, which deep down we long to hear."

"Sometimes I ask for guidance to help me make a decision, but I don't seem to get an answer," said

Christopher. "What should I do then? Is it best to take no action at all?"

Eric closed his eyes for a moment. "'...*Sit by and ask to have the answer given you,*' it says in paragraph 5.[40] 'Sit by' implies wait; 'sit on the decision', if that's possible. The ego often leaps in and demands immediate action – fire off an angry email; snap back at your partner when they've said something you think is unkind. If you notice an impulse to do something, ask whether or not it comes from a place of peace.

"The Holy Spirit is patient, but consistent in His message. If you aren't sure how to act, ask for Guidance again and be willing to wait for an answer. Don't demand that it comes right away. Often, the response will show up in an unexpected way, at just the right time: a song playing on the radio; an advert on the side of a bus; a 'chance' phone call from a friend. Guidance takes many forms, but the content – love and joy and peace – will always be the same."

"I've got a question," said Mark. "Paragraph 4 says, '*Throughout the day... tell yourself again the kind of day you want; ... the things you want to happen to you, and the things you would experience?*'[41] Does that mean it's okay to ask for specific things? Like a meeting going well, or a woman saying 'yes' when I ask her out?"

"I think it's fine, but remember, the things you *think* you want will not necessarily give you what you *really* want – which is peace and joy and awareness of your and everyone's true identity as Son of God.

"Perhaps the young lady accepts your invitation, but when the date comes round it ends up being the most awkward two hours of your life."

"Or perhaps she's a zombie," said Christopher.

"That's not very likely," said Eric. He sounded irritated. "When you pray for specifics, you can still acknowledge your willingness to step back and be led. Say, for example, 'Right now, these are the things that I think would bring me happiness. But You know better than I do what would be for the highest good. Therefore, I am content to follow Your lead. Let things be as You would have them be. Where my wishes align with what would extend awareness of Your love and peace and joy, may they come to pass. But where a different set of experiences would enhance or extend awareness of love and peace and joy, I am willing to set aside my own desires for the greater gifts which You would offer instead.'"

Eric stopped talking, a chance to pause and reflect.

Geoff turned to Rav. "You've been very quiet. I'm interested in what you have to say."

The invitation took him off guard. "*'Today I will judge nothing that occurs.'* Which Lesson did you say that is?"

Eric checked his notes. "Lesson 243."

"Thank you." Rav wrote the number in pencil in the margin of his book. "I will use that for the morning activity you suggested. I think it is a very important lesson."

People were looking at him, expecting him to say more. "I have marked a section of the passage we listened to so that I can contemplate it further. In paragraph 2, it says, *'Today I will make no decisions by myself. This means that you are choosing not to be the judge of what to do. But it also must mean you will not judge the situations where you will be called upon to make response. For if you judge them, you have set the rules for how you should react to them.'*"[42]

"What does that say to you?" asked Eric.

"Thoughts come before reactions. If I judge a situation as not to my liking, I may want to take some action to change it. If I am on the bus, and someone is talking loudly on their phone, I may judge this as 'bad' or unsocial… I then ask for guidance on what I should do: do I complain, or do I get up and move to a different seat? But perhaps the situation is not 'bad' after all…

"If I do not judge the situation, I am open to other possibilities… Perhaps I listen to more of the conversation, and I understand why the person is agitated. Staying in a state of peace, I can perhaps spread the Lord of Love's peace to them. Or maybe I hear something that will be useful to me. Or I see something from the window which I would not have seen if I had moved seats."

"That feels like the perfect note on which to break for tea," said Eric. "Do go through to the kitchen and make yourselves a drink. You know where to find everything."

The others got up and headed to the kitchen. Rav stayed seated, until only Eric and he were left in the room. Eric began to rise from his chair, but fell back into it. On his second attempt, he stood up. "Please excuse me for a moment," Eric said.

"Are you all right?" asked Rav, concerned. "Can I do anything for you?"

Eric shook his head, but then stopped and looked straight into his eyes. "Do you remember what you said to me that first evening, when we were doing the introductions: that when we look at each other, we see the same Self?"

"I remember it," said Rav.

"If something going on this body of mine should cause me to lose sight of the Self, will you continue to see It for me?"

Rav nodded.

"Please, hold me in your prayers." Without saying anything further, Eric hobbled from the room.

* * *

"What would you like, Rav?" Daisy asked him when he joined the other students in the kitchen. She'd taken on Eric's role of organizing drinks.

"I will have a green tea if there is any please."

"One green tea coming up." She dropped a teabag in a mug, filled it with hot water from the kettle, then removed the teabag after giving it a very quick stir. "I can't say I like green tea," she said. "It's definitely an acquired taste."

Rav accepted the mug from her with a smile and went to stand by the window. The plant on the windowsill had drooping leaves, some of them starting to yellow. Taking a closer look, he saw the soil in its pot was bone dry. He glanced over at the sink, but Mark and Irene were chatting directly in front of it.

Geoff came up to him. "I hope you didn't mind me singling you out. Some people tend to do all the talking and you never get a chance to speak. I think you've got a lot of value to contribute to the group."

Christopher, standing nearby, overheard. "Rav only talks if he has something worth saying. He's a sage."

Rav brought his drink to his lips, but it was too hot yet to sip. The more he continued along his spiritual path, the less wise he felt.

Daisy, Irene and Mark joined them in the circle.

"Has anyone heard from Katie?" Geoff asked.

"That's a point!" said Christopher. "She wasn't here last week either."

"I'm worried about her," said Geoff.

"It's her concert this week," said Daisy. "At the Festival Hall. I expect she's busy preparing for that."

"Maybe," said Geoff. "Does anyone have her number? I'd like to check up to see how she's doing?"

"Remind me later," Daisy replied. "I think I saved it in my phone."

"The person I'm concerned about is Eric," Irene said. "Has no one else noticed how poorly he looks?"

"I was thinking the same," said Daisy. "All through the meditation he looked uncomfortable. He must be coming down with a bug. It's that time of year, isn't it?

Half of our yoga class were missing this week."

"He hasn't looked well for a couple of weeks now," said Irene. "I hope it's nothing more serious."

"I'm sure it's not," said Daisy.

Rav felt less certain, particularly after what Eric had said to him, but he didn't feel it was his place to say more.

After a pause, Geoff asked, "Are there any biscuits?"

Daisy shook her head. "I must bring a pack next time. It's unfair to expect Eric to buy them every week."

Rav began to wonder how he might politely extricate himself from the group and attend to what Eric had asked, but Daisy touched his arm. "Are you married, Rav?"

"Yes, I am."

"Do you have children?"

"Not our own. We did used to foster."

"Oh, that must have been rewarding?" she asked.

"Yes, quite rewarding."

"But sad when they moved on?"

"A little sad, yes."

"Why did you stop fostering?"

"My parents became older. We had to look after them."

"I liked what you shared before the break," Mark said to him. "About your experience on the bus."

"You can learn a lot on buses," Rav said.

"Aren't you ever tempted to judge?" asked Geoff.

"Oh yes," he replied. "Frequently. When this happens, I remind myself the price of judgmental thoughts. How can I judge anything and still be at peace? I cannot. How can I judge a person and at the same time perceive the Lord of Love in him? It is not possible. I cannot. When I realise the negative affects my judgments have on me, it sometimes helps me to surrender them. Sometimes though, it does not help." He smiled.

"Well, that's a relief to hear!" Christopher said. "I had you down as an enlightened master. You and Eric as well. Although, did you notice how Eric snapped at me? He's obviously not a fan of zombie movies!"

"I am very sorry," said Eric. He stood in the kitchen doorway, clutching the inside of the door frame. "I'm afraid I'm not feeling myself this evening. I think I'm going to have to cut short tonight's session. Would you all mind?"

"Oh, Eric..." Daisy went up to him. "We thought you might be unwell. Is there anything we can do?"

"Thank you, but no. I feel what I need is an early night."

"Yes, of course," said Irene. "Have you taken some medication? Would you like me to pop to the chemist and get you something?"

"No, Irene, thank you. That's a kind offer but, please, I just need to get some rest."

"Let's go," said Rav, putting down his cup.

"What about the washing up?" asked Daisy. She walked over to the sink and reached for the rubber gloves.

"Leave it, please," said Eric. "I'll put it in the dishwasher in the morning. Really, I'll be fine. I'll contact you all about next week."

One by one, they filed out of the kitchen. Daisy gave Eric a hug. Geoff patted him on the shoulder. Rav hung back until the others were out in the hallway, putting on their shoes and coats. He had the sense that Eric was nearing the end of his journey. That thought made him sad. *'Today I will judge nothing that occurs,'* he reminded himself silently.[43]

"Aham Brahmasmi," Rav said to Eric.[44] "Your real Self cannot be threatened, as the Course I think would say."

"Aham Brahmasmi," Eric affirmed.

6

Katie

What a morning! Katie took her coffee and made her way to the quietest corner of the staff room. Poor Maeko would never be able to play the violin. The girl had no interest in learning an instrument and probably as little aptitude for music as any other child Katie had taught. If she passed her Grade 1 retake it'd be a minor miracle. Her parents were only tormenting her by insisting she carry on.

Katie fished her phone from her handbag. No new messages, but she did have some emails. She opened the app to view them.

Half a screen of new ones since she'd checked in at breakfast, most of them junk. She opened one from the dating app: *Keith wants to get to know you.* Really? He must be the wrong side of fifty, she thought, glancing at his photo. Still, at least give him credit for being honest… With most of them, their profile picture is a decade old and photoshopped to boot. *Keith enjoys gardening and crosswords.* He sounded like a granddad too. She felt slightly guilty as she tapped the trash can… But if she replied to every one of them it'd be a full-time job.

Your car insurance policy expires soon. Yippee, another bill. *Your renewal quote is £479.97.* What? Seriously? Where was she supposed to magic *that* from? Last year, it'd been three hundred and something. Why did they keep hiking her premium when she'd never made a claim? She'd have to go on a price comparison site to get a better deal; another thing to add to her to-do list. You'd think they'd make an effort to hang onto their customers with a half-decent quote. And she had the cost of Christmas to think about as well.

Your ACIM Thought of The Day. Oh, go on then. She opened the email. *Lesson 268: Let all things be exactly as they are.* You're having a laugh, right. She smiled at the thought of Jesus getting a sky-high motor insurance renewal quote.

Next in her inbox, an email from Geoff Hooper with only *"Hi"* in the subject line. She didn't know anyone called Geoff Hooper. It must be a scam, but she tapped on it anyway. "Hi Katie. Did you see Eric's message?" At the mention of Eric, she twigged it must be Geoff from the Miracles group. She didn't recall giving him her email address. "…Terrible news isn't it? Hope you don't mind me getting in touch. Just wanted to check you're ok as we missed you the last 2 meetings. Hope you can make it tomorrow."

She went back to her inbox and found the email from Eric. He'd sent it to the whole group, with everyone's address visible.

"Hello everyone. First of all, please accept my apologies for cutting short our session last week. I was in a lot of pain and had to take my medication. One of the side effects is that it completely knocks me out.

"It's time I was open with you. Two months ago I was diagnosed with cancer of the liver. On Monday I saw my consultant. He told me that it's spread. His diagnosis is I have weeks, not months.

"Back in October when we started meeting, I had hoped I'd be well enough to run the group for the whole eight weeks. I still want to do that, but we'll need to make arrangements one week at a time. There's talk of me moving to a hospice, but I hope not just yet. My daughter is coming over from New Jersey next week, and the thought of enjoying some time with her in my home keeps me going. The problem is I have so little energy, though the nurse who visits me has been a tremendous help.

"Tomorrow night's session is on as normal, and it would give me great pleasure if you can join me. I want to focus on forgiveness.

"Please don't worry about me. And please, if you come tomorrow, don't make a fuss. *'Nothing real can be threatened.'*[45] That means, nothing which Love created can come to harm. My body represents an idea I've identified with for a while. But what I am in truth is not my body. God is Love, so there is nothing to fear. I am at peace.

"With love and light to you all. Eric."

Katie rested her phone in her lap. Poor Eric. *Cancer.* And there was she getting worked up over disinterested pupils and the price of her insurance.

She should probably go to tomorrow's session. No, she wanted to, to show support. She wondered whether to take him flowers. He'd said he didn't want a fuss. But if no one brought him flowers, that wouldn't feel right. She thought about getting him lilies – the Course talks about 'lilies of forgiveness'. But then she remembered you take lilies to funerals. Perhaps an orchid: something beautiful which would last longer than a few days.

"Ah, Katie!" The Deputy Headmaster loomed over her, making her jolt and splash some of her coffee on her dress. "Free period?"

"Yes," she said. He had a knack of making her feel guilty. "My first one this week."

"Is everything okay? You look as though there's something on your mind?"

"No, everything's fine."

"Good," he said. "Splendid. That's what I like to

hear. I've a little favour to ask, actually. It shouldn't require much of your time…"

She felt her nails dig into her palms.

* * *

During the opening meditation, Katie twice caught Geoff flirting with her. The second time she returned his glance with a frown. It felt inappropriate, when they'd only yesterday found out about Eric having cancer. This wasn't the night.

After about five minutes, Eric began to speak. "I've wondered sometimes if *A Course in Miracles* might have been called A Course in Forgiveness. It tells us that forgiveness is our function (Lesson 62); that it's the key to happiness (Lesson 121); that it offers everything we want (Lesson 122). Those are bold statements. Forgiveness is fundamental to the Course's teaching.

"But before we go any further and explore what forgiveness is, I first want to clarify what it isn't. It's another familiar word which the Course uses in an unfamiliar way.

"In the world's eyes, to forgive a person means to pardon them for some wrongdoing. Their action caused us hurt but, because we're nice people, because we're charitable, we deign to forgive them. They're guilty and deserve condemnation, but instead we overlook their offence.

"In the Course," Eric continued, "forgiveness is something very different. It's a letting go of judgment, which helps us to see one another as we really are. It's the prerequisite for recognizing our oneness with our brothers and God." He reached for some sheets of paper and handed them to Katie. "Would you take one and pass the rest on?"

Katie saw he'd set out some quotes from the Course.

"Take some time, silently, to read these extracts,"

Eric said. "Stop to reflect at the end of each one. You might pause after every sentence to let it sink in.

"A friend of mine, when she reads a Lesson or a section of the Text, imagines she's reading a personal letter sent to her from Jesus. Perhaps you'd find it helpful to visualise that? What does he want to communicate to you, in your life right now, through these words? What would he have you know?

"We'll take a quarter of an hour over this. As the Course says, *'there is no hurry now, because you are using time for its intended purpose'* – which is to awaken from time to eternity and remember what you are."[46]

* * *

"Irene," said Eric, "would you like to read out one of the extracts? Choose a quote which you want to explore."

"I'm not sure I understand the first one: *'Forgiveness recognizes what you thought your brother did to you has not occurred. It does not pardon sins and make them real. It sees there was no sin. And in that view are all your sins forgiven. What is sin, except a false idea about God's Son? Forgiveness merely sees its falsity, and therefore lets it go. What then is free to take its place is now the Will of God.'*"[47]

Eric nodded. "I think the key to unlocking it lies in the question, *'What is sin, except a false idea about God's Son?'* To have a false idea is to believe something which isn't true. So perhaps the first question to ask ourselves is, what *is* the truth about God's Son? Does anyone have thoughts on that?"

"I thought God's Son was Jesus?" Irene asked, sounding unsure.

"It's not only Jesus," Katie corrected her. "It's all of us."

"Yes, or all creation, to broaden it out even more," said Eric. "Turn to the section *'What is Creation?'* in the

Workbook." He took his copy of the book and found the page. "It comes immediately after Lesson 320. *'Creation is the sum of all God's Thoughts, in number infinite, and everywhere without all limit. Only love creates, and only like itself. There was no time when all that it created was not there. Nor will there be a time when anything that it created suffers any loss. Forever and forever are God's Thoughts exactly as they were and as they are, unchanged through time and after time is done.'*[48]

"Then, in the third paragraph, we read, *'Creation is the opposite of all illusions, for creation is the truth. Creation is the holy Son of God, for in creation is His Will complete in every aspect, making every part container of the whole. Its oneness is forever guaranteed inviolate; forever held within His holy Will, beyond all possibility of harm, of separation, imperfection and of any spot on its sinlessness.'*[49]

"So, the Son of God shares God's qualities. What God creates is eternal. It's changeless. It can't be harmed or suffer loss. And Its sinlessness is assured.

"When we look at somebody and see anything *but* the eternal; anything *but* the changeless; anything which can cause or suffer harm, we're not seeing the truth of who they are. We've had a false idea about God's Son. Does that make sense?"

"But people do terrible things," said Irene. "You can't deny there's evil in the world."

Katie looked at Eric, wondering how he'd answer Irene's question.

He waited some moments before he responded. "The Course acknowledges that. It says, *'the world was made as an attack on God'*.[50] The world's very purpose is to witness to our separation from God, Who is Love, so is it any wonder it can appear so fearful?

"The statement, *'Forgiveness... sees there was no sin'* [51] seems problematic, when every day our senses witness to the contrary. We only have to pick up a paper or watch the news. But it might help our understanding to rephrase the sentence slightly. It could as easily read,

'Forgiveness sees there was no separation'. In the Course, sin – which is the effect of a lack of Love – is synonymous with separation from God. You might say that cutting ourselves off from God was the original sin, from which arose all the rest.

"Forgiveness as the Course teaches it is merely the realisation that 'ungodliness' is impossible. *'There was no sin.'* [52] Why? Because there was no separation from God. We think we cut ourselves off from Him, but we never left our home. We couldn't have, because nothing exists apart from God.

"Yes, bodies can hurt bodies. That's what we see in the world. Egos can wound egos. Every day we experience that. But Spirit cannot harm Spirit. What God created must forever be a part of Him. And what is part of Him must share his essential qualities: If God is Spirit… If God is Love… If God is innocent… If God cannot harm or be harmed… The same must hold true for God's Son, who is a thought in His mind."

Katie thought about Anne, the girl who'd killed herself at school.

"Katie." Eric made her jump. "Would you like to read out another of the extracts?"

She chose the next one on the page. "This is from Lesson 122. *'What could you want forgiveness cannot give? Do you want peace? Forgiveness offers it. Do you want happiness, a quiet mind, a certainty of purpose, and a sense of worth and beauty that transcends the world? Do you want care and safety, and the warmth of sure protection always? Do you want a quietness that cannot be disturbed, a gentleness that never can be hurt, a deep abiding comfort, and a rest so perfect it can never be upset? All this forgiveness offers you, and more…'*"[53]

"Okay, pause there." Eric stopped her. "Does anyone have anything they want to share on that?"

"It sounds like heaven!" Daisy said.

"I know when I think of someone I hold a grudge against, my body tenses up," said Christopher. "I certainly don't feel peaceful."

"Indeed," said Eric. "There is no peace without forgiveness. But remember, what this is describing isn't forgiveness as it's commonly understood. Listen to the next part. Katie, will you carry on?"

"*'Forgiveness lets the veil be lifted up that hides the face of Christ from those who look with unforgiving eyes upon the world. It lets you recognize the Son of God...'*"[54]

Eric raised his hand to stop her again. "This is about being aware of the Truth beyond illusions. When it talks about *'the face of Christ'*, that's the true Self, God's Son.

"It's one thing to say someone made a mistake. But to look with unforgiving eyes is to hang on to any thought which judges; any thought which resents or feels aggrieved. Do that, and we're reinforcing our belief that someone or something 'out there' can threaten us. At the same time, we're denying our True Reality, as well as theirs.

"Okay, Katie, please read the last bit. I won't interrupt you again!"

"*Here is the answer! Would you stand outside while all of Heaven waits for you within? Forgive and be forgiven. As you give you will receive. There is no plan but this for the salvation of the Son of God...*"[55]

"*'...Today it will be given you to feel the peace forgiveness offers, and the joy the lifting of the veil holds out to you...*"[56]

"*Forgiveness offers everything you want. ... Let not your gifts recede throughout the day, as you return again to meet a world of shifting change and bleak appearances. Retain your gifts in clear awareness as you see the changeless in the heart of change; the light of truth behind appearances.*"[57]

"The gifts it's referring to are the peace of God and joy which touches on bliss. The 'world of shifting change and bleak appearances' is what the psalmist called the 'valley of the shadow of death'. Though we walk through that valley, we fear no ill, because God is with us and we are safe in God. We see the 'light of truth behind appearances'; we meet the eternal in the temporal... That's what it means to forgive."

Mark raised his hand and waited for Eric's nod to speak. "The first part of what Katie read reminds me of the line in the Lord's Prayer: *'Forgive us our trespasses as we forgive those who trespass against us'*.[58] 'Trespass' is an old-fashioned way of saying sin. I realise now that it's not God who forgives us, because God didn't condemn us in the first place. It's we who need to forgive ourselves and see the truth that we're innocent. That we're worthy of love.

"If I judge another person as sinful, or unworthy of love; or if I see them as merely their body, I'm going to think of myself in the same way. I mean, I can't believe that I'm the Son of God while I deny that you are too – because the Son of God encompasses *all* of us... It's only when I see the truth in another that I'll be able to recognise the truth about myself."

He spoke hesitantly, but his words were coming from a deep place. There was something authentic about him which she found attractive. A pity he didn't seem interested in her.

"How does this work in practice?" Geoff asked. "We can talk about seeing people as innocent, seeing only the good in them. But if they've hurt us... I mean, really hurt us? What would you say to someone who's struggling to forgive?"

Eric took a deep in-breath, then exhaled. "I would say, first, give up the struggle. Forgiveness is the Holy Spirit's function, so hand it over to Him by bringing your darkness to the Light; by asking for His help to let go of unforgiving thoughts. Our role in this is to be *willing* to forgive. In other words, are we prepared to ask for help in relinquishing our own judgments and the identity we've built around being a victim and feeling aggrieved?"

Geoff continued to frown.

"We might not be ready to forgive someone for *their* benefit," said Eric. "But are we willing to forgive for *our own*? We can focus on how they've mistreated us and continue to be 'right'. Or we can seek help in letting those thoughts go – because we want to be happy; because, though we've been hurt in the past, we no longer want to continue to be hurt in the present. Do we want to keep the wounds raw? Or are we ready to let them heal? That's the choice we have to make."

"Sometimes it's hardest to forgive ourselves." Mark voiced Katie's own thoughts.

"Yes, absolutely. Rav, would you like to read the last extract out for us? The one from Lesson 228?"

"'*My Father knows my holiness. Shall I deny His knowledge, and believe in what His knowledge makes impossible? Shall I accept as true what He proclaims as false? Or shall I take His Word for what I am, since He is my Creator, and the One Who knows the true condition of His Son?*

"'*Father, I was mistaken in myself, because I failed to realize the Source from which I came. I have not left that Source to enter in a body and to die. My holiness remains a part of me, as I am part of You. And my mistakes about myself are dreams. I let them go today. And I stand ready to receive Your Word alone for what I really am.*'"[59]

"Thank you. Really, forgiveness of self and forgiveness of another are the same. There is only one Son of God, so wherever we see sin – whether we project it outwards or see it in ourselves – we're hanging on to that 'false idea'. Again, we don't actually have to forgive. We only have to be *willing* to forgive – which means to see things differently, as those lessons early on in the Workbook taught us. Once we're willing, we can ask the Holy Spirit for help.

"Pain and guilt go hand-in-hand with our belief in separation and isolation from God. But we never left our Source. And if we think we harmed another, it was only because we forgot what we are and, in that state of forgetfulness, we made a mistake. But those mistakes don't change God's Love for us and don't alter the truth of what we are. No more do they alter the truth about the person we may have hurt.

"Here's a quiz question for you… No looking at your books! Which lesson title is so central to the teaching that it features in the Workbook three times? Do you give up?"

"*'God is but love and therefore so am I?'*" suggested Mark.[60]

"Not quite, but it's a good guess. It's actually very close: *'I am as God created me.'*"

Daisy looked it up in the contents. "Lesson 94," she said. "…Lesson 110… And Lesson 162!"

"Maybe Jesus ran out of fresh ideas," said Christopher.

Eric smiled. "If we believe we can alter, or destroy, or tarnish what God created, are we not in effect saying we're more powerful than God? And isn't that the height of arrogance, however we dress it up? So it isn't humble to feel guilty. It isn't modest to feel unworthy. But nor is it a sin! It's simply a mistake… a false idea about the Son of God. And that, my friends, is the Course in one lesson."

"Or in three," said Christopher.

Eric raised his eyes to the ceiling in mock exasperation. He looked genuinely happy, thought Katie. Completely at peace.

7

Christopher

"This may be our last meeting together," said Eric, bringing the period of silent meditation to an end. "So I want it to be fun. And it gives me great pleasure to have Emma, my daughter, join us this evening. I hope that's okay with everyone?"

The woman smiled and waved. Christopher had been wondering why Eric would let someone new join the group when they'd already met together for six sessions. Hearing she was his daughter, it made more sense. He'd put her in her late forties, a fair bit older than Mark or Geoff. Her chestnut-coloured hair had started to grey.

"In a moment," said Eric, "I'm going to hand out some paper. I'd like you each to take a slip and write down one question you have about the Course. Don't put your name on the paper, just your question. Then I'll ask Emma, my glamorous assistant, to collect the questions and I'll draw them from my hat one at a time."

Christopher took a piece of paper and passed the rest on to Katie. He chewed on his biro, unable to think what to ask. *What's your favourite ACIM Lesson?* No, that was naff. *What does 'atonement' mean?* He kind of already knew: learning that separation never happened, and remembering our Oneness with our brothers and God. *Why do some people experience physical healing but others don't?*

To ask Eric that now would be too close to home. He sneaked a glance at what Katie had written.

The others were handing in their slips of paper. Hurriedly he scribbled something down.

Eric rummaged in his blue football hat.

"You're not a Millwall fan?" Geoff asked, aghast.

"In my younger days."

Christopher sniggered. Eric, a Millwall supporter! He'd never have imagined that.

Eric pulled out a piece of paper which had only been folded once, so thankfully not Christopher's question. "*What does the Course say about kindness?*" he read. He shut his eyes, seeming in no hurry to respond.

Christopher wondered if he should try Eric's approach at his next job interview when the panel asked a tough question: fall silent, close his eyes and ask the Holy Spirit for a prompt!

"The word doesn't appear very often in the Course," Eric finally said, "but to truly live what the Course teaches *is* to be kind.

"Kindness is an aspect of love. It's love in action. It's love expressed in the world. In the Bible, in Galatians, it's one of the fruits of the Spirit. Kindness happens effortlessly when we let ourselves be led by the Voice for God.

"It does say in the Workbook, '*Love created me like itself… Kindness created me kind*'. [61] When we don't show kindness, it's because we've listened to the wrong teacher and lost touch with our true Self. Guilt, fear and judgment get in the way of us expressing our kindness. All of those come from the ego. The ego isn't capable of kindness… It may have us *pretend* to be kind, but only to get something in return. But our ego isn't what we are.

"Kindness and judgment are mutually exclusive. When we're judging someone; when we're seeing them as simply their body, or as their ego, we're not being kind to them. We're also being unkind to ourselves. We experience the effects of our own judgment… a lack of peace; feelings of isolation and guilt.

"But if we hand over our judgments to the Holy Spirit and let His be the eyes with which we see, we'll be freed from thoughts which stop us being kind. In awareness of our True Nature, guilt and fears fall away.

"If someone studies the Course but continues to be as unkind as they were before, then either they haven't understood what they're reading – or they're not applying it. They'd be better off putting the Course down and finding another path. We can't enter heaven on our own. That's basically saying that we can't experience real joy and peace without being kind.

"OK? Ready for another question?"

"Go for it," Christopher said.

Eric read out the next one: "Why does *A Course in Miracles* always refer to God in the masculine?"

That would have been Irene's question, Christopher thought. Or maybe Daisy's. He'd seen what Katie had written, so he knew it wasn't hers.

This time, Eric didn't need to seek guidance. "God isn't male *or* female. Neither is the Holy Spirit or Christ. Gender is an aspect of form, not of Spirit. It's part of our identity in the world, but it isn't our Reality.

"I think the masculine is used for expediency. If the Course referred to God in the feminine, some people might find that a barrier too – they might think it significant that the female gender had been used. If you find the male pronouns unhelpful, then ditch them. But try to see beyond the pronouns. We're talking about Being rather than *a* being. We're talking about Is-ness. Keep the focus on that."

"You don't get away with it that easily," said Eric's daughter. "I've another question. Why does the Course talk about our brothers all the time? Why doesn't it say, 'brothers and sisters'?"

"Well," Eric replied, "I think that's for a similar

reason. I suspect, if it referred to 'brothers and sisters' we might focus on male and female *bodies*. It would draw our attention away from the fact that we're talking about our brothers *in spirit* – and our oneness with them in God. 'Brothers' clearly encompasses everyone; the whole of creation in fact. If you want to substitute 'brothers' with 'sisters', do. But the Course is about seeing each person as they really are – which is beyond male or female or any physical characteristic they have."

"It's like that line in the Bible," Mark said. "In Christ, there is no male or female, there is no Jew or Gentile; there is no slave or free…"

"Indeed," said Eric. "I think that's Galatians again. We're all one in Christ, which is our eternal Self…" After a pause, he pulled another piece of paper from his blue woollen hat. As he read it to himself, his forehead creased. "I'm not reading this one out," he said.

"Oooh," said Daisy, "we're intrigued now. What does it say?"

"I'm not sure it would be appropriate." He put the paper to one side on the table. "That's not what this evening is about."

Christopher felt his pulse quicken. Surely it couldn't have been *his* question which Eric refused to read out. Unless he'd had a humour by-pass in the last week! *Not what this evening is about!* So much for fun.

Eric moved on to another question. "*Is there anything in the Course you disagree with?*"

That had to be Geoff's question, for sure.

"Yes," said Eric immediately, making Christopher sit up. "The punctuation. Whoever edited the Course didn't know the difference between a semi-colon and a colon. Or maybe they got it wrong on purpose to present a forgiveness opportunity to pedants like me! But, to be serious, do I believe everything *A Course in Miracles* teaches is true? I start from the position that the highest truth is Love. Love expresses itself as kindness; as forgiveness, or non-judgment. It lays down no conditions. It's experienced by the giver as Joy and a sense of Peace.

"Since the Course is all about *'removing the blocks to the awareness of love's presence'*, I find it a powerful signpost to Truth. If I'm visiting China, I might see a signpost by the side of the road. But that sign will only be helpful to the extent that I understand what's written on it – if I don't know the Chinese language, it won't be of any use to me. I think it's like that with *A Course in Miracles*, or with any spiritual or religious teaching for that matter. I need to understand not only the language, but also the spirit in which it was written. Otherwise I'll misinterpret it, and perhaps apply it in an unhelpful way.

"I'll give you an example." Eric reached for his copy of the book. "Lesson number 136. *'Sickness is a defense against the truth'*. If I read it without discernment, I find it problematic… *'Sickness is a decision. It is not a thing that happens to you, quite unsought, which makes you weak and brings you suffering. It is a choice you make, a plan you lay, when for an instant truth arises in your own deluded mind, and all your world appears to totter and prepare to fall. Now are you sick, that truth may go away and threaten your establishments no more'.* [62]

"In other words, we're so afraid of our Oneness with God that, to reinforce our belief in having a separate identity, a part of our mind engenders illness and pain. We do this unconsciously. We do it even to the point of physical death, which 'proves' we were right; that separation is real.

"Immediately my ego objects to that. What about babies with life-threatening conditions? Or, for that matter, kind and decent people who are diagnosed with a terminal illness in the prime of their lives? To say that, on some level, they chose disease can sound uncaring and cold."

"Abhorrent too," Daisy chipped in.

Eric continued, "We need to be wary of trying to

interpret any line in the Course in isolation. Often the meaning becomes clear only when we consider it in the context of what comes after or before. Later in the same lesson, the Course gives an explanation: *'You can but choose to think you die, or suffer sickness or distort the truth in any way. What is created is apart from all of this. Defenses are plans to defeat what cannot be attacked. What is unalterable cannot change.'* [63] Bodies are figures in our dream which witness to separation. And sickness too denies our Wholeness. But these witnesses are false. Within the dream, bodies get sick and die, but the truth of what we are continues as it always has been. God thought us into being and we remain, as Spirit, in God's Mind. As God is eternal, so are we.

"When I study the Course, I can listen to one of two inner voices. If I listen to the part of me that delights in separation, I react against what I've read – or I may accept it on a superficial level, but don't let it touch me and affect how I live. If I allow the Holy Spirit to interpret the words, then I see them in a different light. Problematic passages begin to make more sense.

"It's my continuing identification with the body – mine or another's – and my belief that it's real which makes the Course's teaching so hard.

"My true Inner Guide can also show me when to share a particular teaching with another person – and when it would be kinder *not* to use words. Yes, sickness is *'a defense against the truth'*, but it's part of our experience in this world. Those who suffer need compassion. In any case, purest truth isn't found in words, but in kindness. There, we've come back full circle to kindness!

"So let me show compassion for those experiencing physical or emotional pain. Let me acknowledge that pain is part of the human, physical, condition. But let me also hold in my mind an awareness of Spirit; of the Divine Essence in all which is beyond pain and death. And let me trust that my unspoken faith in a person's

Wholeness will, on some level, reach their soul."

"That's beautiful," said Daisy. She'd not been her usual talkative self.

"Shall we do another question before we break for tea?" Eric delved again into his Millwall hat. "My, that's a difficult one," he said, reading the paper he picked. "*What's your favourite biscuit?!*" He looked straight at Christopher.

So that question earlier which Eric refused to answer hadn't been his. Christopher fought to remain poker-faced. "Why are you looking at me?"

"Well, for whoever asked, there's no contest. A dark chocolate digestive wins every time. And, by the way, thank you for reminding us not to take this all too seriously. The Course says that our problem is less that we had a *'tiny mad idea'* [64] of being separate from the Whole, but that we forgot to laugh at that idea and instead took it for the truth."

"Okay," said Christopher. "I'll take the credit. I asked about the biscuit because I couldn't think of a proper question. But I've thought of one now…"

"Ask away," said Eric.

"Aren't these ideas dangerous? Couldn't they be used to justify all kinds of things? I can rob you in the street, but, hey, it doesn't matter because it's only a dream. We can continue to pollute the planet and not have to worry because, you know, the world's an illusion anyway. I'm not saying that, but some people might."

"And if they did," replied Eric, "they would have fundamentally misunderstood what the Course says. Yes, with every spiritual teaching, we need to guard against it being misinterpreted. The ego is quick to jump in and hijack an idea for its own ends.

"But, as I said before, if in doubt, let kindness be the test. I can study the Course for thirty years, memorise all the lessons so I can reel them off one after the other, but if I routinely act in an unloving way, it's a sure sign that

I've missed the point. We demonstrate what we truly believe by how we act."

Christopher had been waiting for a pause to come back in. "Okay, I get that with the robbery example. But with climate change, it's not only the wilful destruction of the planet that's the issue. It's complacency. It's people like you and me and others like us recognizing there's a problem but not doing anything about it… not taking steps to change our lifestyles, I mean drastically change them, which is what we need to do.

"'*The world was made as an attack on God*', so we don't have to worry about looking after it," he added.[65] "Isn't it dangerous to propagate that idea?"

Eric nodded. "That line you quote is another which would be very unhelpful if we took it out of context. It's an emotive statement, and people – even most Course students – are likely to misunderstand it. So let's tone the language down and say that the world is a stage on which we play awhile at being separate individuals."

"All the world's a stage, and all the men and women merely actors," said Rav, quoting Shakespeare.

"You ask an important question though," Eric continued. "I'd say, with any lines like that, if you're not sure how to apply them, or if they feel out of kilter with the highest truth – which is Joy, Peace and Love – seek the Holy Spirit's guidance… And if you don't know whether the guidance you're getting is authentic, let kindness be the check. If the thoughts which come to you make one person out to be more valuable than another, or exclude anyone from the circle of compassion, those are tell-tale signs they're not from God.

"Why don't we try it now? Let's go within and ask for guidance. How can we – you and I – respond in a loving way to climate change? Ask the Holy Spirit in quiet. Have a paper and pen to hand, so if anything comes to you in the silence you can write it down."

* * *

"Okay," said Eric, "Would anyone like to share what came to you?"

To begin with, no one volunteered. Christopher certainly wasn't reading his, not that he'd written very much. Hesitantly, Irene raised her hand. "I don't know if this is right," she said. "I'm not sure if it's in line with what the Course teaches…"

"Why not read out what you've got?" Eric encouraged her.

"If you're crossing a road and suddenly a car comes racing round the corner, you don't say 'that car is an illusion'. You get out of its way! You do what needs to be done. If we have a headache, we take a pill for it. If we're unwell, we see a doctor. And if the earth is sick – and it is, because the world reflects the disharmony in our minds – we do what we need to, to ease the symptoms of that sickness.

"If we're unwell because we have high cholesterol, we need to stop eating fatty foods. If the planet is unwell because of pollution, we need to stop pumping chemicals into the atmosphere and plant more trees."

"Thank you for sharing," said Eric. "I think that's absolutely right. I'd only add that those solutions focus on addressing the symptoms. They're necessary: as you say, we need to relieve the symptoms. But there's also the underlying cause, the disharmony you mentioned. I might say more in a moment, but is there anyone else who'd like to share what they wrote?"

"I can," said Daisy. "But I want to say first what a remarkable experience that was, asking the Holy Spirit a specific question. For a couple of minutes, nothing much happened. But then I had a thought… And I wrote it down. And then, before I finished writing the sentence, another thought came. So I wrote that as well.

Words simply flowed onto the page, as fast as I could write. I've never experienced anything like it before. Anyway, here goes. I've not had a chance to read it back to myself yet, so I don't know how much sense it'll make…

"While we live in the world, let us live with love, with kindness. What sort of world do we want to inhabit? Let's be the change we want to see.

"There is only one Son of God, so we're all interconnected. We're one with our brothers and sisters wherever they are. And, because the Son of God is outside of time – is not only everywhere but also 'everywhen' – what we think of as future generations are one with us too. The decisions we make now will affect how life is experienced fifty, a hundred, five hundred years from today.

"Some things we can do right now, like choosing an energy supplier which only uses renewable sources like wind or solar power. But beyond that, we will each be called to contribute to the healing of the world in different ways. Let us discern what action we each can take that would extend peace and joy.

"For some, our call may be to get involved in active campaigning – though with love and forgiveness always at the forefront of what we do. Others among us will be called to heal the world first and foremost through inner work. Minds are joined,[66] so when we heal ourselves, we help to heal the Whole." She glanced up at Eric. "I'm not sure about the last bit," she said.

Wow, Daisy, thought Christopher. Where did *that* come from, old girl?

"Wonderful," said Eric. "I think it's spot-on. The word 'healing' also came to me very strongly… I felt guided to Chapter 27 of the Text, 'The Healing of the Dream', and to the Section called 'The Healing Example'.

"I read, in the first line of that section, *'The only way to heal is to be healed.'* [67] Then, in the same paragraph, *'No one can ask another to be healed. But he can let himself be healed, and thus offer the other what he has received. Who can bestow upon another what he does not have? And who can share what he denies himself? The Holy Spirit speaks to you. He does not speak to someone else.'* [68] That appears to be at odds with what the Course says elsewhere: the Holy Spirit *does* speak to everyone, but I think what it means in this passage is that we can't count on another person's readiness or willingness to listen to that Voice. *'Yet by your listening His Voice extends, because you have accepted what He says.'* [69] You used the word 'interconnected', Daisy. And I think when we accept healing; when we accept ourselves as God created us, that's going to contribute to healing in ways we couldn't plan.

"The other line which leaped out at me was: *'A dying world asks only that you rest an instant from attack upon yourself, that it be healed.'* [70] 'A dying world.' That's very stark; and it works on two levels – on the level of individual lifeforms, and the planet as a whole. Whenever we behave in an unloving way, we attack ourselves, because all is One.

"I had the image of a cat fighting its reflection in the mirror. We laugh at the cat, but we do the same thing when we send out unloving thoughts. So let's stop attacking, stop trying to judge everything by ourselves, and instead let's *'Come to the holy instant and be healed'*, as it says here. [71] The holy instant is an instant, mediated by the Holy Spirit, in which we experience Wholeness. It's a moment in time when we stand outside of time and bear witness to eternity. *'The holy instant's radiance will light your eyes, and give them sight to see beyond all suffering and see Christ's face instead. Healing replaces suffering. Who looks on one cannot perceive the other, for they cannot both be there. And what you see the world will witness, and will witness to. Thus is your healing everything the world requires, that it may be healed.'"* [72]

* * *

When they broke for coffee, Christopher jumped up to beat the rush for the bathroom. Returning, he found the sitting room deserted. Laughter came from the kitchen.

As he passed by the table next to Eric's chair he noticed the slips of paper, one of them apart from the rest. He'd forgotten all about the 'forbidden question' which Eric hadn't answered.

Christopher heard Daisy's voice in the kitchen above the rest, and then the whistle of the kettle coming to a boil. He glanced over his shoulder.

Pulse galloping, he grabbed the question and read it…

"Caught in the act!" said Katie, behind him.

He spun round. Where the hell had she sprung from?

"What does it say?" she asked in a whisper, walking up to him. "Spill the beans."

He handed her the paper and watched as she read it: *'This is not a question for Eric, but for Katie. Will you go out for a coffee with me?'*

"Hmm!" was all she said.

"Do you know who wrote it?" Christopher asked her, curious.

"Well, I don't think it was Rav, do you? Maybe Daisy wrote it, what do you reckon?"

Christopher shrugged. "Mark?"

She frowned a little and shook her head.

"Who else could it be?" he asked.

"Geoff. Obviously!"

Christopher thought about it. "But Eric's already read out Geoff's question. The one that asked if there's anything he disagrees with in the Course. I'm sure Geoff asked that."

Katie huffed. "Well, it's a mystery then, isn't it?" She sounded irritated. But then her eyes flickered and a mischievous smile appeared. "He won't get an answer unless he asks it to my face."

8

Daisy

Daisy stood by the parking-meter. Three pounds for up to two hours. Five pounds for up to four. She hesitated. A couple of hours would be plenty, surely. Except, she didn't want to be looking at her watch. She unzipped the loose change compartment of her purse. Not much in there... Two pound coins, but she needed one of them for the locker at the gym. A couple of fifty pence pieces. She emptied the rest of the coins into her palm and counted up the twenties and tens. Two hours it would have to be.

Placing the ticket in the window of her car, she began to doubt if coming here had been such a good idea. What would she say to him? What *could* she say that would help? *Don't be pathetic*, she told herself. The main thing is to show that she cared. She straightened her hair, using the shiny brass plaque at the entry to the drive as a makeshift mirror. St Clare's Hospice. It'd been thirty years since she'd visited Daddy, God bless him, in a place like this.

The baskets of pansies hanging from the porch roof were a nice touch.

She approached the reception desk where a young woman sat thumbing her phone. "Hello, Beata," she said, reading the woman's name badge. "I'm Daisy

Lloyd. I'm here to visit Eric Painter."

"Good morning, Mrs Lloyd," she replied with a heavy accent – Polish, Daisy guessed. "Eric expects you. He is in sun lounge. I show you to him."

She followed Beata along a corridor, past a forlorn Christmas tree. A bit sparse, she thought: a few red and gold baubles here and there, and plain white fairy lights. It looked half-finished; no care or imagination put into its decoration. The residents deserved better than that.

Perhaps Beata read her mind. "Garden centre donated for us lovely tree this year, so we put it in lounge. Eric and his grandson helped to decorate. Perhaps later he shows you."

"Oh, I'd love to see it." Daisy chastised herself for her judgmental thoughts.

When she spotted Eric, she nearly stopped in her tracks. How gaunt his face looked. How pale.

He raised a hand and smiled. "Daisy, it's lovely to see you. Forgive me if I don't stand up."

"Hello, Eric," she managed, doing her best to sound bubbly. She stooped to hug him and to kiss his cheek. "I do like your fleece. It feels very snug. The green suits you."

"A present from Emma, my daughter."

"I met her at the group. Two weeks ago."

"Of course. Please, sit down."

Daisy drew up a rattan chair.

Beata hovered. "You like I get you something to drink?"

"What do you fancy, Daisy?" Eric asked.

"I'd love a tea, thank you."

"Sugar?" asked Beata.

"Half a spoon."

"Tea for me as well please," said Eric. "Two sugars." He winked at Daisy. "I can indulge my sweet tooth as much as I like now."

"That reminds me, I brought you something," Daisy

said, handing her carrier bag to Eric.

His face lit up as he peered inside. "*Premium biscuits half coated in rich Belgian dark chocolate and sprinkled with coconut*," he read aloud from the box. "You remembered my favourite."

"We've Christopher to thank," Daisy said. "Otherwise I wouldn't have known."

Eric's smile broadened. "I'll have one with my tea. Or maybe even more than one. How are you?" he asked, after a pause.

"Okay," she said. She should be asking him that question, but fear of the answer prevented her. "This seems a nice place. It's very quiet."

"It's certainly that. No noisy neighbours here playing the drums until one in the morning. I'm sorry," he said, noticing her reaction. "The nurses are friendly and look after me well."

"Beata told me your grandson helped decorate the Christmas tree?"

"Emma and I probably enjoyed that more than Danny did! The last time I dressed a tree I couldn't have been much older than he is now."

What else to talk about? "How's the food here?"

"Oh, they spoil us. It's like staying in a hotel. At home, I cycled through the same few meals: beans on toast; chips and beans; beans with pasta. Eric's speciality, that. The chef here does the most delicious roast potatoes."

Daisy turned to take in the garden. "The lawn is well-kept."

"Look!" He pointed. "On the feeder. See the robin?"

Together they watched it until it flew away.

"I enjoy watching the birds," said Eric. "There's a big wood pigeon who perches on top of the feeder. He knows there's food inside, but he can't quite fathom how to get at it. Just between you and me, I'm not sure he's very bright. Ah, I managed to get a smile out of you!" After a moment he asked, concerned, "What's wrong, dear? Are you *really* okay?"

She felt tears welling in her eyes. "It's so unfair. You should have another ten years of life, at least, to be able to enjoy your retirement."

Eric leaned forward and took hold of both her hands. "Look at me. Look at me, Daisy. What is it you see?"

She saw a man who was dying. A man just a few years older than her.

"What do you see?" he repeated, softly.

"You," she said. "My friend. My teacher." Perhaps he wanted more from her, but she couldn't say it. She pulled back a bit and he let go of her hands.

"It's okay," he reassured her. "I'm not in pain. Look in my eyes. Don't be frightened. Can you see that I'm at peace?"

"I see that," she nodded, then reached in her bag for a tissue. "It's me who's the emotional wreck."

"You're upset because you see something that isn't there.[73] You see my body, a dying body, and that makes you sad."

"You might recover," she interrupted him. She didn't believe it, or he wouldn't be in this place, but she had to cling to the hope. "Doesn't the Course say, *'there's no order of difficulty in miracles'*?[74] You hear about people who experience miraculous healings. Don't give up. We must never give up."

"Daisy, hear me. I'm not giving up anything that's real, only my identification with this body; only a false idea of what I am. That's what healing is. It's not about curing the body. It's about letting go of false identifications."

"How can I...?" She dabbed at the corner of her eyes with the tissue.

"Go on," he encouraged her.

"It feels so selfish to be troubling you with questions. I was going to ask, how can I be as okay with this as you are? You're my friend. How can I not be sad?"

"Daisy, first of all, it's wonderful to have you as a friend. And it's okay to feel sad. Don't hold back if you want to cry. To recognize our pain is a first step in healing. When we allow our emotions, we can look at the thoughts behind them. Only then can we ask for help to see things another way."

"I don't want to lose you."

"You can't lose me, Daisy. You can't lose me, because the truth of what I am is what you are as well. What we lose, we never had, but only *dreamed*." He stopped as Beata approached, carrying a tray with two cups.

"Tea with two sugars is cup on left."

"Thank you," replied Eric. "Beata is an absolute angel," he said to Daisy, but loud enough for the woman to hear as she walked off. "In Polish, her name means 'blessed', or holy. What a beautiful reminder of what we are."

"Can I ask you something? Are you really okay with dying? Aren't there things you're going to miss?"

He sighed. "If I think I'll be leaving Emma and Danny behind, or my friends, I do feel sad. But more and more, I'm at peace. It depends on which teacher I choose to listen to in any moment. When I feel afraid, when I feel a sense of loss, that's my cue to ask the Holy Spirit for help. He reassures me, over and over, that nothing created by God can be threatened and nothing which God didn't create is true. [75] So I'm not my body. I'm not the roles I've taken on: dad or granddad, teacher of the Course, friend. Only what God created is my Real Self; and what He created has no end.

"There's a lesson I keep returning to. *'God is still Love, and this is not His Will'.* [76] That doesn't mean sickness or death shouldn't be happening. It means they *aren't* happening in reality – in the Mind of God – but only within our collective dream. When I think something shouldn't be happening, that's a judgment. It's resistance. But when I trust in the Voice for God, Who tells me the body isn't the Self which God created, it opens the way for forgiveness... Only forgiveness offers peace."

Four months later

By the time Daisy extricated herself from the phone call with her sister, her watch showed one minute to seven. Poppy was such a chatterbox! Natter, natter, natter about everything and nothing. It meant Daisy hadn't time now to make herself a tea. She scurried up the stairs and switched on her laptop before taking a seat at the dressing table which had become her desk. The screen stayed blank. As she was about to press the button again, a message popped up: *Windows is installing updates. Please wait.* "Oh, fiddlesticks!" she exclaimed. Of all the inconvenient times. She hated to be late.

When she finally logged in and started up Zoom, all the others had already joined the call. "Hello everyone!" she said, waving. "I'm sorry to be late."

"Hi Daisy," said Christopher.

"Hi," said Katie, waving back.

"How are you?" asked Rav.

"I'm fine, thank you. I'm doing okay." Daisy took in the familiar faces, happy to see them again. "How's everyone coping with the lockdown?"

Irene appeared to be saying something. "You're on mute, Irene, dear," Daisy said.

"Is this better? Can you hear me now?"

"Yes," Daisy replied. Christopher gave a thumbs up.

"I've still not got the hang of this technology," said Irene. "If my son wasn't home from university to help me, I'd be lost. What a crazy situation! It's terrible, isn't it? Every day I hear the statistics and there doesn't seem to be an end to it in sight."

"But what the stats don't tell us is how many people have had it and never been tested," said Geoff. "For most people, the symptoms are relatively mild. Katie's had it."

"What, you've *had* the virus?" asked Irene, beating Daisy to it.

"I'm pretty sure I did," said Katie. "I had a fever and a horrible cough. It's okay, I'm recovered now. Still isolating, but I'm feeling much better. Exhausted, that's all. I sleep for twelve hours a day."

"Do you have everything you need?" asked Mark. He'd grown a beard, which made him look older. "Food? Medicines?"

"Yes, I've got enough at home to keep me going, thanks," replied Katie. "Geoff's been bringing me supplies and leaving them on the doorstep. He's playing the part of doting boyfriend very well."

"Boyfriend?" asked Daisy, surprised.

"Sorry, we should've said. Geoff and I are an item! We've been going out since January."

"Congratulations!" said Daisy, echoed by Rav and Irene.

"Good for you," said Christopher.

Geoff beamed. "It'll be our three month anniversary tomorrow. Though I've been missing the cuddles these last couple of weeks."

Katie smiled. "Yeah, cuddles are difficult when you have to stay two metres apart!"

Daisy saw someone's screen go black. Mark's video had gone off.

"I'm really worried," said Irene. "Aren't you frightened too? I mean, this pandemic may go on for months. And if we do get through it, what's the economy going to be like? I'm genuinely scared."

"Can I read something from the Course?" asked

Daisy. "It's a short lesson. The first part is a prayer. It's helped me see the situation differently…" She saw people nod. "It's Lesson 244: 'I am in danger nowhere in the world.'

> *"Your Son is safe wherever he may be, for You are there with him. He need but call upon Your Name, and he will recollect his safety and Your Love, for they are one. How can he fear or doubt or fail to know he cannot suffer, be endangered, or experience unhappiness, when he belongs to You, beloved and loving, in the safety of your Fatherly embrace?*
> "And there we are in truth. No storms can come into the hallowed haven of our home. In God we are secure. For what can come to threaten God Himself, or make afraid what will forever be a part of Him?" [77]

"Amen to that!" said Christopher.

"It's a nice prayer," Irene said. "But I *am* frightened. People are dying, and there's still no cure. They reckon it'll be next year before there's a vaccine. So we *are* in danger. Surely?"

"Are *you* worried, Rav?" Geoff asked, before Daisy could respond to her friend.

Rav unmuted himself. "One of my daughters is a nurse. I do worry for her. But what does worry achieve? In these days more than ever, it is important to choose peace."

"How do you *choose* peace?" asked Daisy.

"I'd be terrified if I had a daughter working in a hospital right now," said Irene.

Rav took his time to reply. "What is that line in the Course…? 'We don't need to seek for love. We need only seek for the barriers within ourselves that we have built against it.'[78] Peace is like love. It is our natural state. My task is to let go of whatever thoughts block peace from my awareness. I will give an example. At the start of the lockdown, I spent a lot of time watching the news: *Channel 4 News, News at Ten…* one after the other. After a couple of days, I noticed something. Watching the news for longer than I need to fuels my fear. But…" He raised a finger. "What is it that fears? It is not my true Self.

"In the title of the lesson Daisy read, the first two words are 'I am'. *'I am in danger nowhere in the world.'* But what am I? What is this 'I am'?" Rav paused. Daisy thought of Eric, the way he'd often break off speaking as he sought guidance on what to say. "The virus appears to threaten us, but remember the line Eric has quoted for us many times: *'Nothing which is real can be threatened.'*[79] This prayer speaks of our Self, our essence. Here, it is called God's Son. God's Son is safe. Always safe. When I become aware I am safe in God, not separate from God, I realise there is nothing to fear."

"How do we get to that awareness?" asked Katie. She looked as rapt as Daisy. "How can we experience that peace?"

"It is already here. Listen. In the silence. In the stillness. *'The soul finds peace in its own source.'*[80] Before I do anything else each day, let me take the time to be still. Let me dwell in the presence of the Lord of Love. When I dwell in that place, I come to know my Self again."

"In John's gospel, Jesus used the same words," said Christopher. "'*I am* the light of the world', he said.[81] '*I am* the way, the truth and the life.'[82] '*I am* the vine, you are the branches.'[83] Those lines always used to bother me, particularly where he says, 'No one comes to the Father except through me'.[84] But now I'm studying the Course, it makes sense. I don't interpret it as Jesus putting himself on a pedestal and saying he's different from us. He's talking about his true Self, the Christ. The Christ Self *is* the way, the truth and the life. And that Christ Self is in us too. We're *all* God's Son. Of course," he added, "that goes out the window when I'm down to my last roll of toilet paper because everyone's been panic buying, and I see my neighbour getting out of his BMW with about six months' supply!"

Geoff laughed. "You should've asked him if he could spare you a roll!"

Daisy was about to share her story about trying to book a supermarket home delivery slot, but Christopher spoke again. "You've been very quiet, Mark," he said. "Are you still there?"

"Yes, I'm here," Mark replied. He still had his video turned off.

"How are you managing?" Christopher asked him. "What's your take on all of this?"

"Well," said Mark, "it sounds strange in the midst of a pandemic, but this can be a time healing if we use it as an opportunity to choose again. All my adult life I've pursued external goals to help me feel happier, but the things I've aimed for are sticking plasters at best. They only address the symptoms and not the underlying problem, which is that I've lost sight of what I am.

"If I identify with what's vulnerable – with my body – then I'm bound to feel fear… It may be a low-level anxiety; most of the time it's hidden beneath the surface, but it's always going to be there. The pandemic simply brings it to the fore.

"That's why the current situation can actually be a help. When things are going okay, when I'm coasting along, I think I can manage by myself and I've little motivation to turn to God. But at times like this, it brings into sharp focus how inadequate my own efforts are.

"All the things that give us a false sense of security or self-worth: possessions, special love relationships, even our own bodies... Suddenly we see how flimsy and fleeting they are. This 'self' we've made up and everything we've built around it is like a child's sandcastle on a beach. It could be corona virus today, or something else tomorrow, or next year, or in thirty years' time. But the tide *will* come in and wash it all away."

"What a depressing thought," said Irene.

"For me, it's not depressing," said Mark. "It's a comfort, because it shows me I was wrong about myself all along. I'm *not* this body. Would God create us as bodies that suffer and die? God is Love and that *can't be* His Will."

Daisy recalled the similar line from the Course which Eric had shared with her in the hospice.

Mark continued, "I've been turning to Him much more these last two weeks. I sit with the Course and open it as I'm guided, and spend time contemplating a paragraph or two. Or I watch one of John Butler's videos on YouTube. [85] They're a great way to begin the day and ground me in my Real Self; in the Peace of God. It might only be for a few minutes, but when I lose my self in the Whole, I 'rest untroubled'[86] and forget my own concerns."

"You and me are lucky," said Geoff. "We don't have to go out to work, so we can use this lockdown as a stay-at-home retreat. But what about people on the front line, like Rav's daughter? Or the supermarket cashiers and shelf-stackers? Or even Katie, who volunteered to go into school to look after key workers' children before she got ill? It's easy for the rest of us to talk." Daisy sensed a challenge in his tone.

Silence now felt awkward and Daisy wondered what to say to break it. The story she'd intended to share no longer felt appropriate.

Katie came to her rescue. "What the nurses and doctors are doing – and other people who are putting their lives at risk to serve others – that's a way of expressing love. They're working miracles, you might say. Hopefully, when this is over, people will value them more. But I think what Mark is saying – sorry, Mark, if I'm putting words into your mouth – is that there are different ways to help? We all need to follow our Guide. Some will be called to carry on doing their vital jobs, being selfless on a practical level…"

They might feel they don't have any choice, thought Daisy, if they've bills to pay and children to feed.

"Others might be called to volunteer; maybe to go to the shops for vulnerable people who can't get out. For some, their task now may simply be to keep themselves safe so they can serve the world another day, in other ways, when their time comes. But the inner work which Mark describes is important too."

Rav was nodding. Geoff had a perplexed expression.

"What the world needs at this moment is healing," Katie said. "I've discovered John Butler too, Mark. He's wonderful, isn't he? So soothing, the way he speaks. I love how he puts it: *'To make whole, be whole'*. To be whole is to be at one with all – and that's a state of consciousness we let envelope us, rather than something we strive to achieve. The Course says the same: *'When I am healed I am not healed alone'*.[87] We've seen with panic-buying how quickly fear spreads. But peace can spread too, from one mind to another. So to heal ourselves isn't selfish. And if that's the task we're given, we've a big responsibility… If we spend our days watching box-sets, then we're not playing our part. Maybe if we're freed from other responsibilities, it's so we can use the time to work on healing our minds of thoughts of separation and guilt. To shed our self: isn't that what being self-less is? It may even be the most important thing we accomplish in our lives."

Mark's video came back on in the bottom right of the screen. Before he'd looked serious, even morose. Now a warm smile lit up his face.

NOTES

1. W-pI.136.18:2.
2. See W-pI.181. The actual title of the lesson is "I trust my brothers, who are one with me."
3. See the first of the Quaker 'Advices & Queries'. (*Advices & Queries*. London: Britain Yearly Meeting, 1994.)
4. T-1.I.9:1-3.
5. T-1.I.5:1-3.
6. T-1.I.45:1-2.
7. T-1.I.24:1-4.
8. T-In.2:2-3.
9. W-pI.109.
10. W-pI.109.2:1-2.
11. W-pI.109.2:3-4.
12. W-pI.109.2:5-6.
13. W-pI.109.3:1-5.
14. W-pI.51.2:2-4.
15. T-27.VIII.6:2.
16. W-pI.54.1:2-5.
17. T-20.VII.9.
18. See T-29.VII.1:9.
19. Matthew 13:45-6.
20. T-16.IV.6:1.
21. T-16.IV.6:1-2.
22. T-In.1:8.
23. T-16.IV.6:2.
24. W-pII.1.4:1,3.
25. W-pI.34.3:2-5.
26. W-pI.34.4:1-2.
27. T-In.2:2.
28. See T-In.2:4.
29. W-pI.14.
30. T-In.2:2-3.

31. W-pI.125.
32. T-14.III.16.
33. T-30.I.1:1-2.
34. T-30.I.14:1-4.
35. W-pI.95.11:2.
36. T-30.I.1:5.
37. T-30.I.4:1-2.
38. T-5.II.3:2.
39. T-5.II.7:1-4,7.
40. T-30.I.5:3.
41. T-30.I.4:1.
42. T-30.I.2:2-5.
43. W-pII.243.
44. Aham Brahmasmi is a term used in Hindu philosophy which translates as "I am the absolute". It describes the unity of the individual self, atman, with the Absolute, Brahman.
45. T-In.2:2.
46. W-pI.rIV.in.7.3.
47. W-pII.1.1:1-7.
48. W-pII.11.1:1-5.
49. W-pII.11.3:1-3.
50. W-pII.3.2:1.
51. W-pII.1.1:1,3.
52. W-pII.1.1:3.
53. W-pI.122.1:1-6; 2:1.
54. W-pI.122.3:1-2.
55. W-pI.122.6:1-5.
56. W-pI.122.11:2.
57. W-pI.122.13:1,3-4.
58. Matthew 6:12.
59. W-pII.228.
60. See W-pI.171-180.
61. W-pI.67.2:4.
62. W-pI.136.7:1-4.
63. W-pI.136.11:4-7.
64. T-27.VIII.

65. W-pII.3.2:1.
66. W-pII.336.
67. T-27.V.1:1.
68. T-27.V.1:6-11.
69. T-27.V.1:12.
70. T-27.V.5:5.
71. T-27.V.6:1.
72. T-27.V.6:5-7:1.
73. W-pI.6.
74. T-1.I.1:1.
75. This is a paraphrase of T-In.2:2-3.
76. W-pI.99.5:5.
77. W-pII.244.
78. See T-16.IV.6:1.
79. T-In.2:2.
80. Maitri Upanishad.
81. John 8:12.
82. John 14:6.
83. John 15:5.
84. John 14:6.
85. See the YouTube channel 'Spiritual Unfoldment with John Butler'.
86. See W-pI.194.9:2.
87. W-pI.137.

Unless otherwise attributed, all quotes are from A Course in Miracles, copyright ©1992, 1999, 2007 by the Foundation for Inner Peace, 448 Ignacio Blvd., #306, Novato, CA 94949, www.acim.org and info@acim.org, used with permission. T at the start of a reference denotes the Text of A Course in Miracles. W denotes the Workbook.

A PERSONAL MESSAGE FROM THE AUTHOR

Dear reader,

In Chapter 8, I included a quote from John Butler. As far as I know, John has never studied A Course in Miracles and there are differences between his teaching and that of the Course. Nevertheless, through his words and, more, through his embodiment of peace and joy, it is clear that he abides in that state of mind to which faithful study of the Course may lead us too.

When I sit down to write, my prayer is that my words be authentic. I pray, too, that they will reach those who they would help.

I hope that, in these pages, you have found something that is helpful to you – whether it be to clarify a Course concept, or to reinforce what you already knew, or to encourage or inspire.

If you did find this book helpful, I ask you to consider taking five minutes to leave a short review or reflection on Amazon.

With kind wishes and blessings,

Peter

By the same author

ESCAPE TO REDEMPTION

Only her own forgiveness can set her free.

Josie only had the gun to frighten Curtis Rook, but his son disturbed her. One startled reflex and now he's dead. Josie flees to Poland leaving her boyfriend Snaz to take the rap. A reformed criminal offers her refuge from the police and the chance to begin a new life, but she cannot hide from her guilt. As the stakes rise, Josie begins to realise that only her own forgiveness can set her free.

Fast-paced and original, Peter M. Parr's contemporary take on *Crime and Punishment* challenges traditional ideas about guilt and redemption, and the meaning of forgiveness.

REVIEWS & ENDORSEMENTS
FOR ESCAPE TO REDEMPTION

"Let me state, very simply, that I loved this book... It is a highly addictive, unique story which raises questions of morality, loyalty and the power of forgiveness. ... With twists in the most unexpected of places, I had to remind myself to breathe. ... What drew me to both main characters was that neither was presented as wholly good or bad. They were rich, complex figures who generated mixed emotions throughout every chapter. ... **Escape To Redemption** is truly unputdownable. It's soulful crime fiction which will leave you asking what kind of person you are when the chips are down. 10/10." – *Sarah Ryan, Cultured Vultures.*

"...Parr's superb understanding of the way human beings justify their sins (especially to themselves) make Josie and Snaz utterly convincing and compelling. An engrossing, realistic morality tale." – *Kirkus Reviews*

Paperback: ISBN 978-1-78535-227-0
E-book: ISBN 978-1-78535-228-7

By the same author

REFLECTIONS ON GOD'S LOVE

Prayers and Inspirations

Reflections on God's Love is a collection of prayers and commentaries to recall our hearts and minds to the loving Presence of God.

The readings provide doorways into contemplation and can serve as inspirations to help us dwell in the Vine (John 15:4-6) and grow in our trust in God. Many of them draw on much-loved Bible passages. Included are reflections which shed fresh light on the Lord's Prayer and on the parable of the prodigal son.

"Father, I have wandered from You long enough. Let me come to my senses, look (at where my wandering has led me), listen (to the inward longing which is calling me home) and return my heart and mind to You."

Printed in Great Britain
by Amazon